CW01497381

Materia

Magica

A Compendium of many of the Various Materials used in the Practice of Practical Magic, With some examples of their use.

Compiled By

Draja Mickaharic

Lulu Inc. Raleigh, NC
USA

First Published in 2010
This edition published 2013
By Lulu, Inc.
3101 Hillsborough Street
Raleigh, NC 27607

www.Lulu.com

ISBN: 978 – 1 – 300 – 88983 – 0

LCCN

Printed in the United States of America

Preface

Dedicated to my Former Students,
As I am no longer teaching

With a special kind word to
Dr. Eoghan Ballard, PhD
Who I first met as a young boy,
and who has grown into a serious
scholar of Magic and Folklore.

§

AN IMPORTANT PRELIMINARY NOTE:

Many of the Latin Binomials, which identify the specific plant scientifically, have been obtained from 'J. M. Nickell's Botanical Ready Reference' The numbers alongside most of these plants refer to paragraphs in this book. This 1880's handbook, 'Especially Designed for Druggists and Physicians' has become a standard in the magical community, and through its reprinting in 1972 and 1976, it has become very well known to later generations of both herbalists and magicians. I am especially happy to see that it is still in print, now sold by the Enos Publishing Company of Banning California.

The scientific community keeps changing their minds concerning the proper Latin Binomials, and as a result, these binomials may not be the binomials used scientifically today. However, as no one can keep up with the continually changing minds of the confused masters of intellectual science, these are the binomials most used among serious magicians. It is for this reason I have included them in this work.

D. M.

I should also add, that the healing uses of herbs as mentioned herein have been abandoned because they have been found not to be effective. Please avoid trying to medicate yourself with herbs; see a physician, his products will work better and faster to heal what ails you.

ACKNOWLEDGEMENTS

In all fields, we stand on the shoulders of those who have gone before us. I owe any success I have had to my teachers, as well as what I have learned through my own experience. It is from these sources this, and all of my other books have been written.

Draja Mickaharic

I should like to add that anyone finding this book useful should also purchase Ms. Catherine Yronwode's excellent "Hoodoo Herb and Root Magic." Despite the fact that our opinions differ in a few places, her book is an excellent guide to the practice of the most popular form of American folk magic. I refer to it constantly, and if you are a serious worker, I am sure you will as well.
DM

Added in 2013 - One of the things one must do when preparing for their demise is to go through all of their accumulated trivia and decide which is to be kept, and which is to be cast aside. That led to the discovery of this long neglected notebook I wrote for my own information in the sixties and seventies. The information is still valuable, so in the hope you could make use of it, I have added it here.
DM

CONTENTS

A

AB RA   The words mean 'Of Ra.' Ra was the name of an Egyptian Deity. I know of no product of this kind, which would have a correct formula from ancient Egyptian times.

ABSINTHE   (Artemisia Absinthium)   delightful liquor, often thought to be toxic if made one's sole beverage. Said by some to reduce the inhibitions. See Wormwood.

ABRAMELIN   Incense and Oil. Supposedly taken from the well-known "Book of the Sacred Magic of Abramelin the Mage." As there are several versions of this book, there are quite probably several versions of the oil and incense. I should be suspicious of any product carrying this label that was not sold in conjunction with a reference to the book. I suggest researching the oil in the version of the book, you are using and making your own oil.

ACACIA FLOWERS   [Acacia Vera]   [#24]   {Pseudo Acacia} Flowers Gum Resin   Called Egyptian Thorn, it is the source of Gum Arabic, often burned for protection. Acacia was considered sacred to the Egyptian god RA. The Acacia tree was once called the "Tree of Life."

Used as an incense for protection, for blessing, and occasionally, for gaining astral power. This last use is very doubtful in my opinion. The powder may also be used as glue.

The herb itself is an initiatory symbol of resurrection, and eternal life, especially as found in Freemasonry, as well as in ceremonial Magical Lodges with a Masonic base, or bias, such as the Golden Dawn, and its many offshoots.

ACONITE [Aconitum Napellus] [#54] See Wolfsbane. A toxic narcotic, not recommended for use.

ADAM AND EVE ROOT   [Aplectrum Hyemale] [#216] (Adan Y Eva) Putty root, often used as a love charm, when made up in pairs by a root worker. One is given to each of the lovers, to be carried by them. The supposedly male root is named the Adam root; the supposedly female root the Eve root.

Ruled by Venus, the roots may be used singly for attaining desires, by praying over it and placing it somewhere near the desire to be attained, or near a symbol of it. It is best used for this purpose in purchasing land or a desired house, if there is any real possibility of the desire actually being attained. The root should be prayed over, and placed, or buried, on the property desired.

The prepared Incense, Oil, Bath Salt, Water, and Perfume, as found in most occult stores are of little value. As the binding spell, connecting two lovers, is one of Venus and Saturn, the herbal blend of Artisima and Comfrey, or other herbs of these qualities, in an Alcohol and Copal base would do as well for the foundation of these products as anything else. The spell must always be prayed over, naming the two names of the people to be bound together. The best incense for this purpose would be Copal Gum Resin. The best water for this purpose would be a mixed tea of Dandelion flowers and Gardenia flowers. This mixture would not have a strong scent, but it would be magically effective.

ADDERS MOUTH   (Stellaria Media)   [#2225] Chickweed, which see. To stop slander, pray over the whole plant and cast it on the slanderers doorstep. An excellent

A

remedial tonic may be made from chickweed, while the fresh leaves are a good addition to salads.

AESCULAPIUS   Oil and Water   Named for the Greek Deity of Healing. This oil is used in the sick room and for healing spells. Green colored Glycerin with any healing herb specific to the patient's condition may be used as an oil in this case. In the water a tea of hearts ease, with some carnation perfume added would be appropriate.

AFRICAN GINGER   (Zingiber Officinale)   [#2463] Ginger, which see. A curse breaker, hex breaker, and blood purifier, it stops Hexes and Curses. The tea is said to cure sore throats. It heats the system, and is good for those suffering from chills. It is a specific for motion sickness. The tea is a warming agent and a systemic tonic. The root is used as a charm under the pillow to cure sore throats, but I prefer the tea.

AFRICAN Ju-Ju POWDER   (Ju Ju Africano)   This is a generic name for any powders made in accordance with any of the African Ju Ju, magico religious or magical Practices. It is not one specific powder, although it is often thought to be. In West Africa, Ju Ju is a generic name covering any one of a wide variety of both initiatory and non-initiatory Christian, Pagan, or Islamic, magical and magico - religious practices.

AFRICAN VOODOO   (Vu Du Africano)   Powder, Oil, Incense, and water.

This is a generic name that has been applied to the products from a specific set of magico - religious practices. While this name could cover anything in this book, there is no one specific powder that is used for such work. The correct name for this rather complex and complete magical religious practice of African origin is Voudon. Voudon is as much of a religion as is the Lutheran Church, Roman Catholicism, or any other religion. It is much maligned by the ignorant that believe it is a religion of the primitive and ignorant. An interesting magico religious practice, it is of benefit to its believers.

MATERIA MAGICA

AGAG AGAR   White Powder   (Gracilaria Lichenoides) [#1097]   Ceylon Moss   The extract gum is used as a bacteriological culture medium and glue. It is infrequently used as ncense in magical operations.

AGARBATTI CHANDAN INCENSE   This Hindu phrase means "Religiously Pure Sandalwood Incense." Again, this is often thought to be a special magical incense, which it s not.

AGRIMONY [Agrimonia Eupatoria] [#83] In a bath, or in a homeopathic dilution of the flower, it can be used to release fears from people. It may also be burned as an incense, to release a fear or terror vibration from a place where a (usually violent) death, crime, or other tragedy, has occurred. The herb is also burned in rituals to reverse evil spells and to free someone from negative work of all kinds.

Known as liver wort, as are many plants of the genus Hepatica. It was used in former times to treat diseases of the liver. It is an astringent, and its tea settles the stomach. Also known as cocklebur, or stickwort, it is usually not a welcome plant when it is found in the garden.

In negative magic it may be used to induce fears in others.

AGUE WEED (Ague Root) [Aletris Farinosa] [#95] Unicorn Root. Ground to a powder, and prayed over, it is to be sprinkled in the path of an enemy, to cause them to become confused and hesitant, (or at least uncertain) in their actions.

May also be used in a cleansing by another, or it may be carried on the person, to break a hex that may have been laid on the person. It may also be burned as an incense, to break hexes, or to stop hexes from being placed. In this case it is used in a fumigation of the person. Magically, it is used to confuse people, or to remove confusion from them, this last is its use in a cleansing. Best as a powder, or a tea from the powder.

It is also made into a bitter tonic that is used for female complaints.

AJO MACHO Male Garlic A powder made from garlic. The prepared ground garlic powder from the grocery store will

4

work very well here. The powder is used as an incense in fumigation, as well as an ingredient in a number of other incenses. Garlic in any form is discouraging to negative influences. There is also a St. Ajo, or St. Garlic, who is appealed to in prayers.

AL ANIMA SOLA (The Lonely Soul) Incense This maybe of two kinds: An incense made of privet and wormwood used to help spirits cross over to the realms of death.

It may also be incense used to summon a negative spiritual force known as 'The Lonely Soul' who preys on those who are weak, driving them into despair, depression, and even eventual suicide. I personally consider this force too dangerous to work with, as it has a very evil reputation.

ALGIERS FAST LUCK (Suerte Rapido) Perfume Considered to be one of the better lottery and gambling perfumes. I use powdered nutmeg and red pepper in an alcoholic perfume diluent for this product. The perfume was once a commercial product, like Algiers Powder, which was made in Algiers Louisiana (Across the Mississippi river from New Orleans) in the pre civil war – ante bellum - south.

ALGIERS POWDER Algiers powder was the scented talcum powder from the Algiers cosmetic line, formerly consisting of a Powder, an Aftershave, Toilet Water, Bath Oil, and Cologne. It was a favorite export item to the Caribbean Islands in the late nineteenth and early twentieth century, but the company went out of business during the depression of the thirties. Named after the city of Algiers, across the Mississippi river from New Orleans, it was said to be very effective as a magical powder, due primarily to its scent. According to my informant, an old man from Santo Domingo, the powder was a rather cheap cosmetic with a strong odor, adulterated with bits of organic matter. He said it became fashionable to make up a replacement dusting powder when the real article was no longer obtainable, and sell it from the last box a little bit at a time. Herewith is his formula for the replacement article, which he claimed would work as well as the original.

> Pure Vanilla extract - 1 ounce
> Finely ground vanilla beans - 2 or 3 ounces
> Finely ground pure cinnamon - 2 ounces
> Finely ground Patchouli Leaves - 1/2 ounce

Mix with about a pound of talcum powder, letting the material blend for a week or more, while mixing it every day.

This is essentially a cosmetic powder, although its components will assist it in bringing success in both amorous and financial affairs.

ALEHOOF (Nepeta Glechoma) [#1576] Ground Ivy
The leaves are used as a stimulant and a tonic. It aids in the relief of pain. It helps to dispel melancholy when distilled in wine. It is used, along with other herbs, in the relief of female problems. Ruled by Venus, it is useful in lead colic. The tea is said to purge lead and other heavy metals from the system.

ALFALFA (Medicago Sativa) [# none] Herb and Seed
Taken as a tea, it may be used to assist in reducing minor heart problems. Over a long term, it is a blood purifier, but it is not recommended, as garlic is much better, and works much faster, for the same complaint.

The herb is high in mineral content, as well as vitamin K, and enzymes that assist in food assimilation. It aids in the elimination of body poisons, and relieves constipation naturally. It is useful in relation to arthritis, rheumatism, neuralgia, anemia, skin problems, and hardening of the arteries. It may be taken in tablet form, in a tea, or better, eaten fresh in salads.

Magically, it may be burned, and the ashes saved to keep poverty away. There is a specific ritual for this, in which some of the ashes are marked on the body of the person. This ritual must be done by a magician priest, or by one who has the moral authority to perform it. You should be careful you are not transferring your own economic status to the person you are assisting should you decide you can perform this ritual.

A

The dried plant, placed on display in the home, is used to keep poverty out of the house. The spell is more effective, but this is suggested as a useful alternative.

ALKANET ROOT   Used for drawing luck and money when kept in the home.

ALL HEAL ROOT [Valeriana Officinalis] [#2388]   Valerian (which see)   Burned as an incense in the sick room. Or made as a tea, to be used as a sick room sprinkle. Homeopathically it is used as a medicinal, to promote general healing.

I have found it better in promoting an accurate diagnosis of the true condition. In this respect it is like homeopathic Sulfur, (30x and above). Valerian should not be used internally except under the direction of a physician or licensed healer, as it can be toxic to parts of the non-physical system. (See HEAL ALL as well)

ALL NIGHT LONG OIL   An Oil used to dull the sensation of the male sexual organ, so the man using it could copulate with a woman for a much longer time. There are several of these products available at any good drugstore. The man using one of these products should wear a condom so he does not dull the sensitivity of his partner's vagina.

ALL SAINTS POWDER   The closest I have been able to come to this powder is one that is made from All Saints Water. My sole informant explained this process in the following way.

Get holy water from seven churches with saint's names. Place seven drops of each of these waters, on a tablespoon of talc, wood base, or an herb. This powder is used as an uncrossing powder.

ALL SPICE (Pimenta Officinalis) (Eugenia Pimenta) [#948] (Espicia) Oil, Incense   The unripe fruit is harvested to make the spice. The grocery store spice is used as an incense ingredient to promote communications.

The oil used is usually safflower oil, with powdered all spice in it. There is an essential oil of allspice, but it is not usually used, as it is too strong for most people.

ALMOND (Almendra) Oil Pure Almond oil is avail able at health food stores, and is used for making up all kinds of preparations, from massage oils to love oils. It is highly recommended for both uses.

Almond oil is probably the best ingredient to use in making up love oils. It takes a magical charge very well, and holds the charge for a long time without diminishing. However, like most love affairs, the oil does become rancid in time.

Almonds are used in European magic for spells of lust and seduction. In Hindu Indian magic they are used to promote chastity.

ALOE, CAPE Gum resin (Aloe Spicata) [#114] It is used as an incense ingredient.

ALOE Aloe Vera [#81] The primary herb of Islam, it is one of the best-known healing herbs. It is an excellent antiseptic for the treatment of cuts and scrapes.

The juice of the crushed leaf can be used to heal bruises, cuts, and abrasions. The plant juice is also used internally, as a body cleanser, and laxative, as well as for suppressed menstruation, but with mixed effects. Recommended for abrasion, scars, and body spots or blemishes.

As a laxative it helps in cleansing the large intestine. Not recommended for the elderly, or for pregnant women because of its strong action. As a liniment it is useful in the treatment of body sores.

In magic it is used in a bath to develop patience in people. It also can be used to develop the patient submission to the will of God. The variation of result depends entirely on the prayer made over the bath. A quarter cup of chopped Aloe is steeped in a cup of boiling water until the water cools. The mixture is added by straining it into a tub of cool or barely warm water, and prayed over for the effect desired. The person taking the bath then soaks in the tub for fifteen or twenty minutes.

A

Aloe is an herb of Venus and the Sun. It is often burned as incense, with a prayer that the person burning it find love. The ashes are scattered outside the front door of the house, supposedly in an attempt to draw love to the door.

This same herb is also said to draw demons, when added to oil and set for nine days. This is its most doubtful use in my opinion.

The aloes used as incense is more often referred to as Lignum Aloes. It is used as an offertory incense when blended with Musk and Myrtle leaves.

ALSTONIA BARK   [Alstonia Constricta]   [#118]   Dita Bark   Known as Fever bark, the bark is used in malarial disorders, and to treat fever. It is said to aid in the relief of rheumatism.

ALTAMISA   [# None]   The tea is brewed and sprinkled around the house to intensify love, or to eliminate personal problems.

ALTAR   The Workbench of the Magician and Priest. The altar may be as little as the top of a table, or as grand and elaborate as one desires or may be able to afford. A permanent altar is a useful thing for a magician to have, both for his daily devotions to his creator, and as a place to do the work he is called upon to perform.

In the event a spiritually directed altar is desired in the home, lotus root powder could be added to the altar during its construction. If an altar oriented to a particular deity is desired, materials of the nature of the deity could be added. The choice is up to the person who owns the altar. I do recommend that anyone regularly practicing magic have his or her own altar.

ALTHEA   [Althea Officinalis]   [#120]   Leaves and Root Marsh Mallow   Mortification root   Used for its soothing and pain relieving qualities. It may be taken as a tea for sore throat, stomach irritation, or for bowel disorders.

It is used as a salve, and in some poultices, as well as making an excellent vaginal douche. It is used in almost all instances of inflammation. It is also an ingredient in the most popular incenses of conjuration.

ALUM   A white powder drugstore chemical used as an incense of Saturn. Aluminum Ammonium Sulfate, it is useful in its usual chemical formulation.

AMADOU [Boletus Laricus] [#397] Larch Agaric Spunk (The plant is also known as Polyporus Formentarius)   It is excellent for stopping bleeding when applied directly to the wound. When inserted between the nails and the flesh it relieves ingrown toenails.

AMARANTH   (Amaranthus Hypocondriaticus) [#126] Prince's Feather. The leaves are used in piles and in other female problems. It is often referred to as the flower of immortality, and is found at witchcraft funerals, burials, and other death rituals. Ruled by Saturn.

AMBERGRIS   The natural, and very expensive product is the regurgitation of the Sperm Whale. The artificial scent is available, and is as useful as the natural scent.   It is infrequently used as incense in traditional summoning and invoking, more often in the preliminary preparation and purification of the ritual area.

AMBERGRIS (Ambar Gris) Perfume From the essential oil. The commercial product is usually an artificial scent, but the artificial scent is as effective magically as the far more expensive natural product.

AMBRETTE SEED   (Hibiscus Moschetos) (Abelmoschus Esculentus) {Abelmoschus Moschatus} [# 1] Okra Musk Seed. The seed capsules are used as a mucilaginous agent. They are also cooked and served as an offering to Chango, the thunder and lightening deity of the Yoruba Pantheon. The dried seeds may be burned as incense.

A

AMBER (Ambar) True Amber Incense is made from the powder of real amber, the semi precious gem, and is quite expensive. The perfume and oil scents are supposedly matched to the scent of the incense, but that depends on who made them. So far as I know there is no effective artificial amber incense. The true Amber Oil is made from dissolving amber in a solvent. Artificial amber oil has no serious magical use.

AMBER MUSK INCENSE A very expensive incense blend used in ceremonial magic rituals dealing with lust, love, and similar interests. It is usually burned in work to gain total emotional control over others, but it may also be used to set the mood or vibration of a place.

The usual formula is a blend of half and half of amber powder and musk extract powder. The mixture should be allowed to blend for at least a month before use. The incense should be burned on charcoal. Artificial musk perfume powder (Not musk crystals) is almost as satisfactory, and is less than a tenth as expensive, as natural musk oil powder. I know of no substitute artificial amber.

ANCIENT WISDOM POWDER The occult store product is usually wood flour with a rose scent. Occasionally chalk is added, although it is sold in many colors. This powder is used to clarify thinking and clear a muddled mind. It is used to assist people in meditation – something rose water will do quite well.

The following will suffice for the occult store variety,

Two or three pieces of sidewalk chalk ground to a fine powder

One ounce of Orrisroot powder

Ten or fifteen drops of Rose oil, (Artificial rose oil)

Mix well and sift together several times.

ANEMONE, WOOD (Anemone Nemorosa) [#186] The windflower. The poisonous flowers can irritate the skin, and cause a redness to develop. Not recommended for use. Formerly used in working with Air elementals, it is irritating to use.

11

ANGELICA ROOT   [Angelica Atropurpurea]   [#194]
(Archangelica Officinalis) Root and Seed   Known as
Masterwort and Archangel. Ruled by Sun in Leo, it is a
stimulant, but not one that is safely used.

The tea is used as a purifying room sprinkle. Used in
corners and across doorways, as well as throughout the room.
A good sprinkle for general house blessing. Used ritually to
sprinkle to the four quarters to ward off evil.

ANGER POWDER   This powder comes in two varieties,
one to create anger and the other to quell it. I shall give
examples of both.

Variety One, used to create anger and high emotions in
a room or meeting place. It is to be sprinkled around the room,
especially on the floor of meeting rooms. This powder works as
well as the more complex Jumby Bean spell, which is probably
better known. However with this spell, the powder may be
distributed more discretely.

Take a teaspoon each of Red Cayenne Chili Powder,
Black Pepper, Cattail Herb seeds, and Guinea pepper.

Mix them together and allow them to stand for at least
24 hours before use. Then sprinkle the powder on the floor of
the meeting room, after praying over it for the effect desired.
This powder may be diluted with two or three tablespoons of
talc before setting it to stand if desired.

Variety Two is a powder used to overcome these
feelings of anger, and to cool out the angry vibrations in a
room.   The following mixture may be scattered around the
room in the same way as the previous one.   However, this
powder assists in avoiding fights, and acts to clear the head
when experiencing negative emotions.   However it will not
completely counteract the powder in variety one, which will
require a spiritual cleansing of the room to dissipate the thought
forms generated by the angry people.

Again, use a teaspoon of each of the following,
Fenugreek Seed and Table salt. Add this to a tablespoon of
Marjoram, and mix together well in the mortar. Then add a
little talc or another filler powder to suit.

A

ANGER POWDER - Used to create anger and strife wherever it is cast. Placed on a person, it will cause them to become angry with others without any reason. If it is cast on the floor of a business place, it will cause those present to become angry with each other as well as with those who come into the establishment. It is very effective either as a casting or a blow powder. A pinch of this powder under a desk will make an office worker display annoyance to all who contact him, ruining the sweetest temper.

A useful formula for this powder is: <u>Variety Three</u>
> Finely ground red chili pepper - 1 ounce
> Finely ground black pepper - 1 ounce
> Asafetida gum - ¼ ounce

Mix together well in the mortar blending the gum in so that it is completely covered with the dry peppers, and the peppers take the moisture from the gum. Allow to set for a week or so, digesting in a closed container. Then sift together several times, to a uniform fineness. Allow the mixture to blend for another week or more before using. Use only as much as necessary, as a little will go a long way. Do not spill this powder; it draws negative forces without further activation.

ANISE [Hypogon Anisatum] [#1194] leaves (Anis)
The leaves are burned in Voudon work as a power incense. Please carefully distinguish from, Anise seed [Pimpinella Anisum] [#1718] who's seeds are burned or given as an offering to Eurzulie, and to other Voudon Loa and entities. Anise seed Oil is made from these seeds. The oil charges well and is useful in magic. Also carefully, distinguish from ANISE SEED (Illicium Verum) whose seeds are used as incense.

ANISE, STAR Illicium Anisatum [#1204] See Star Anise.
Ruled by Yemmenja, the Sea mother goddess of the Yoruba. An excellent spice for sauces or when cooked with chicken. Used as a charm to promote dreaming.

ANOINTING OIL (Untar) Used to anoint and dress candles, to put on charm bags, ritual instruments, and for other similar magical purposes. Any general purpose anointing oil is of doubtful merit. The following is elevating anointing oil, useful in anointing people.

Orrisroot powder, One ounce; Lotus root powder, and Benzoin powder, one-quarter ounce each. Oil, as shown below, eight ounces.

Mineral oil is used for malefic work, as in candle dressing. Vegetable Oil is best for beneficial work. Cotton seed oil is very good for this particular blend. The oil may be used to bless people, places, or things. It is very difficult to do negative work with this oil.

ANOINTING POWDER   This powder is used to anoint people after they have had spiritual cleanings. The powder allows them to keep their newly raised vibrations a bit longer. I recommend that it not be used too frequently, as it may be too diverting for some people. Apply the powder as a blow powder to the sternum, sacrum, and the cervical spine.

Make the powder from an Ounce of Orris root powder, a quarter ounce each of Lotus root powder, and Benzoin powder. Add talc or a filler powder to suit if desired. After mixing, allow this powder to stand for a week or so before using it.

APPLE FRAGRANCE (Fragancia de Manzana)   The perfume is from the essential oil. According to Jewish and Christian biblical mythology, the apple as a symbol of sexual temptation, was the downfall of mankind. Thus, apple perfume and oil is used as a love and seduction aid.

APRICOT FRAGRANCE (Fragancia de Albaricoque)   The perfume is from the essential oil. In Chinese Myth, the apricot is the fruit of immortality. I like apricots but I do not attribute my long life to eating them.

ARABIC, GUM (Acacia, Arabica) (Acacia Vera) [#24] The gum resin of Acacia, as a powder prepared for use as incense or as glue. As an incense it is used alone for general work, but more often it is used as a slight admixture to other incenses, where it has the effect of enhancing the odor of the other incense. It is protective, and particularly useful in positive work, and worship.

ARAB KA SOUDAGAR INCENSE (Also ARABKA) Myrrh incense, in a poor transliteration from the Arabic. It is supposed to be burned when business is bad to bring luck and money to a business establishment. There are better incenses for this purpose than Myrrh.

ARCHANGEL, White (Lamium Album) [#1289] {Angelica Officinalis} Blind Nettle Ruled by Venus, it is a non stinging nettle. Burned as incense with prayers to bring back a lost love.

ARECA NUT (Areca Catechu) [#241] Betel Nut Tree The tree yields Gum Catechu. The betel nut is chewed, along with powdered lime, as a mild narcotic stimulant. The gum is often used as incense, particularly mixed with sandalwood when working with some of the Asian deities.

ARI SENTHER Another bad transliteration, but I cannot find an original I am certain of. It is supposed to be used in job seeking, employment, and advancement spells, as Van Van oil is often used.

ARNICA (Arnica Montana) [# 256] Wolfbane Common Arnica A poisonous narcotic herb that has great value in treating muscular injuries of all kinds. The flowers are used to make healing salves, baths and massage oil rubs. A handful of the flowers with a quart of boiling water poured over them make the material for the soaking healing bath. Very good for muscular tiredness and strains. The homeopathic preparation, and salve are also useful. The leaves and flowers are occasionally burned as incense, but their use as an incense is not recommended.

ARRACH (Caenopodium Olidum) [#594] A nervine Not much used anymore, as it is not very effective.

ARROWROOT POWDER   (Maranta Arundinacea)

[#1436]   The starch is used in thickening foods, and in diluting powders to be used as magical powders. It has a very bland vibration. A good diluent, it is generally a poor incense.

ASAFETIDA   (Narthex Asafoetida)   [#1563]

Asafoetida   Known as devil's dung to Americans, it is an Indian spice, used frequently to season curries and other Indian foods.

Asafetida is most used in negative magic, what is commonly referred too as black magic.   Mixed with sulfur it makes an incense which is said to draw forth the demons from hell. The incense actually has the property of attracting negative and malicious spiritual entities to its fumes. The proper proportion for summoning negative entities is 40 % sulfur, in the form of powdered flowers of Sulfur, and 60 % asafetida. Thus it is often burned when laying curses on an enemy.

This usually evil incense can actually be used in a spiritual cleansing of a building, but it is important it be used correctly. A large washbasin, the kind of galvanized iron tub used for ducking for apples at Halloween party games, is required. The incense burner is supported in the center of the washbasin, so that it will not tip over. The basin is then filled with water, almost to the level of the base of the incense burner. The charcoal for the incense is lit, and a small amount of asafetida incense is placed on the charcoal when the charcoal is burning evenly. Once the fumes stop rising, the incense burner is suddenly knocked into the water. The washbasin is immediately carried from the place it was burned, and the water dumped into a river, sewer, cesspool, or a septic tank.

The negative entities in the building are drawn to the incense, and then find themselves trapped, or devitalized, by the water in the galvanized iron washbasin. When the incense is put into the water they will usually attempt to chase after it, losing at least some of their force to the water. The water is then dumped into a river, sewer or cesspool, a place that these entities usually find entirely to their liking. They have left the building, and hopefully will not return.

A

According to Gulta work tradition, it is also burned to force someone to leave you alone. I would think that the smell would be sufficient to do this.

ASH LEAVES (Tree leaves and Bark) (Fraxinus Excelsior?) Carried to draw a lover. It may be burned to provide protection to a person. It should be used as an infumation of the person to be protected.

The powder of the bark of the ash tree [#629 ?] is used as a protective tea in a floor wash, especially to keep someone out of the house. The powder may also be used to seal a place against someone, or to get someone to lose track of the user.

The bark and berries of the Northern Prickly Ash (Xanthoxylum Fraxineum) [#2453] {Zanthoxylum Fraxineum} is used as a healing media for sores in the mouth, as well as relief of toothache.

The powder of Ash bark is used for blessing or cursing when scattered or blown to the four quarters. Ruled by the Sun, Ash is the Norse Tree of Life. Ash is the original Indo European word for Tree.

ASTER Aster Puniceus [#313] Venus rules it. The leaves and flowers were used to decorate Druids altars. The root of the aster plant is used medicinally. It is said to be a holy plant.

ASTRAL TRAVEL OIL To be used to anoint a person before astral traveling. In this it would have to be similar to the witch's flying ointments of old. These contained deadly nightshade, henbane, and other things to make the heart race and the pulse pound. These oils are not recommended for either use or experimentation. There are no oils that will allow you to project into the astral realms. This is a mental effort acquired by training and self-discipline.

ATTRACTION (Atrayente Atraccion) A magnetic material, and thus made with lodestone and pulverized iron, known as magnetic sand. The material is used to attract people

17

conditions, and things, into the life of the person using it. A good attraction powder is:

One ounce each of High John the Conqueror powder, and of red Ocher. A half-ounce of Cinnamon, and a half-ounce of Calamus root powder. Expose this powder to the field of a strong magnet for at least three days, preferably a week. If you wish to use a filler powder, add an ounce of talc, to make up four ounces.

AUNT ANNA WISHBONE POWDER   In some of the American conjuring practices, their teacher gives a Magic Wishbone to the person who is to practice the art. This wishbone is usually kept in a clay pot. At the successful completion of the spell, it is fed with a powder, made up for the purpose. This is the wishbone powder. The powder is usually left on the wishbone for seven days, when it is removed, and may be used for dreaming true by placing it between the sheets of the dreamer's bed.

Wishbone powder is a powdered herb or plant powder native to the area where the conjure worker practices. Several plants claim to be the true wishbone powder. Dried and ground Mullin herb seems to be the most common herb used for this purpose.

This happens to be a rather potent and practical means of performing all sorts of magic, although not one in common use or of common knowledge.

AUNT SALLY DREAM INCENSE   Mullein leaf powder has the best reputation for bringing dreams. Adding Sage or Bay Leaf to Mullein can assist in making the dreams more real. Adding Myrrh will help bring the dreams to manifestation.

AUNT SALLY DREAM POWDER   A powder that is sprinkled on the bed sheets, under and around the bed, to bring good dreams. Finely powdered dried Mullein leaf powder is good for this application. A small amount of powdered Myrrh, added to the Mullein leaf powder will assist in manifesting the dreams.

A

AUS   Aus means OUT or Off in German. In southern Germany, aus is a banishing powder made of barn dust (sweepings) and table salt. The powder is thrown at negative forces to drive them away while shouting AUS! AUS! at them.

B

BABEL OIL   A mental confusion oil of mixed effect and reputation. Contains mint and negatively charged Patchouli in a base of mineral oil. May be used as a candle dressing oil, or applied to a trace of the person who is to be confused.

BALM OF GILEAD BUDS   (Populus Candicans)   [#1802] Carried for protection against evil, and also to solve love problems. These are best used for love problems with a current lover or spouse, not for the lack of a lover.

The buds are used for their balsamic and soothing effect. When a tea is to be made, the buds must first be soaked in alcohol to remove the resin.   The tea is a vulnerary, and is beneficial to wounds.   The buds are reputed to be an aphrodisiac when steeped in wine for seven days.   The bark makes a tonic tea. The recovered resin, which is not usually available as a separate item of commerce, makes a fair incense.

BALM MELISSA   (Melissa Officinalis) [#1464] Balm or Lemon Balm   Ruled by Jupiter and Cancer   The herbs and flowers are used medicinally. The salve made from the flowers is supposedly used to increase the size of a women's breasts. I have no experience with this supposed use.

B

BALMONY (Chelone Glabra) [#588] A plant related to figwort. The root is used for powerful hexing spells. The root powder is added to many hexing incense mixtures. You must clearly identify the person to be hexed when you burn this incense against them.

The leaves are a bitter tonic, which taken as a tea, and can be used to expel worms.

BARBERRY (Berberis Vulgaris) [#363] The bark of the root is used in treating liver complaints, the berries are a systemic cooler.

BALSAM (Balsamo) (1) A tree, whose sap is occasionally used as incense. (2) The generic description of the gum or saps of certain trees.

Balsam of Peru is an example of the later. Usually it describes the gum or sap of a tree whose gum was once used in medical practice, often as a natural glue.

BANISHING INCENSE (Destierro) Used in banishing and exorcism rituals, this incense is used to eliminate negative spiritual forces. There are any numbers of incenses used for this, beginning with dragon's blood, which is quite effective for the purpose. Dragon's Blood must be burned either out of doors, or with at least one window open. The fumes carry the negativity off with them.

BASIL [Ocimim Basilicum] [#1591] In the middle ages it was said that crushing basil bred scorpions. The Basil plant and Scorpions are both ruled by Mars in Scorpio. Mars in Scorpio is Mars in a water sign. So we find the strong dynamic energy of Mars directed through the emotional force of water.

Basil is assigned to Oshun in the Nigerian Yoruba pantheon, as Oshun rules all of the strong desires of people, in addition to sex, love, beauty, and money. The same rulership is found in the Voudon practice, where Basil is said to be ruled by Erzulie. Basil is said to be a better herb for women than for men, especially when used as a home sprinkle or as a floor wash.

The sprinkle is also used to draw money and success to a business place.

The energizing effect of Mars found in basil can have a protective and cleansing effect. Basil is frequently used in magic to add a light martial vibration. It has the same protective and cleansing effect in spells it has in teas. A tea of basil may be used in baths, washes, and sprinkles, to give this effect.

Basil used as a flavoring herb is also very good, as it adds this light martial vibration to a person through the food. Traditionally, it is used as a love potion by powdering the dried leaves, praying over them, and sprinkling them on food for the beloved. It is a nervine and stimulant; it aids suppressed menstruation, and reduces the itching of insect bites.

When making pasta sauces, you should add basil in proportion to the oregano you put into the sauce. The correct proportion is a bit less than 1/3 Basil to 2/3's Oregano. In this proportion, the martial Basil balances the feminine vibration of Oregano.

Basil water used as a spray lightens a room. Basil soaked in alcohol can be used to reduce tension in people, when wiped on their back or shoulders. A basil bath has a protective and cleansing influence. In all cases, basil has a protective and lightening positive influence, wherever it is used.

Basil incense does not have as strong an effect as basil used in teas or washes. Because Basil is connected to Mars in Scorpio, water brings out the martial qualities of Basil better than fire does. An example of Basil used in an incense is taking equal quantities of Basil and tobacco, mixing them, and burning on charcoal. It will drive away negative influences from the place where it is burned, and add a mild or gentle protective vibration.

BAST The Egyptian Cat Deity Incense for this deity may be made from Natron (Washing Soda) thinned with oil, and mixed with catnip. This deity is very approachable currently, as many new age people pray to her about their cats. The ancient Egyptian prayer ritual to Bast is quite interesting, and is never,

B

or almost never, followed when these new age people pray to Bast today.

BAT'S BLOOD INK   Used for writing out curses and other negative work. This may be made from Chinese red writing ink, usually available at art supply stores. If desired, a bit of liquid Ox Gall (Also from an art store) may be used to moisten the red ink stone. Use a small Chinese writing brush to write out the message.

The usual formula given, using Dragon's blood, cannot actually produce negative results, as dragon's blood is an incense of exorcism, and is not really suitable for writing out curses, the primary uses of this ink.

BAY LEAF   [Laurus Noblis]   [#1037] Laurel leaves were the leafy crown awarded to the ancient winners of the many Greek games and contests. It is from this that our word Laureate, meaning one who has received an award of laurel, originates. Our kitchen Bay Leaf is the same herb as the laurel leaf of antiquity.

The pythonesses that delivered the oracle at Delphi induced herself into a hallucinogenic state by chewing bay, or laurel, leaves. Because it is a potent and dangerous hallucinogen, bay leaves or berries, should never be ingested (eaten). Mercury rules Laurel, due to its strong effect on the mind.

Medically, a paste made of Bay leaf tea can reduce the sting of insect bites, but as it is toxic, it must not be taken internally.

Bay leaf can be used as an incense, adding a mercurial vibration to an incense compound to help it better communicate with the astral realm. The leaves are not a particularly effective incense by themselves. They can be considered to be a magical expediter for incenses.

In magic, Bay leaf is usually used in wishing spells, as well as an additive to put mercurial vibration into other spells. It is often carried as a protection against evil. It has connection with the Sun in Leo, and is sacred to Apollo.

Bay leaves are thought to be protective against curses, when placed one in each corner of each of the rooms of a house. They are also thought to be protective when carried on the person. One bay leaf placed in a wallet protects your money.

A typical Bay Leaf Wishing spell is to write out what you desire on a piece of paper. Now fold the piece of paper into thirds, and place three bay leaves inside. Again, fold the paper into thirds, and place it away in a dark place. Once the wish is granted you should burn the paper as a thank you. The process of writing out the wish and folding the paper must be done while concentrating on the wish.

The Nobel Laurel, or Bay Tree, is the European version of the American plant following, Bayberry, which has the additional ability of producing a wax used for making candles.

BAYBERRY [Myrica Cerifer] [#1537] (Baya De Laurel) Used in the form of Bayberry candles at Christmas time. They are usually lit with a prayer that they bring money and good fortune in the coming year. Ground bayberry root bark is occasionally used as an incense by itself. As an incense it has a Mercurial and Saturnine vibration. Also see Bay Leaf above.

> Bayberry candles
> Burned to the socket
> Bring luck to the home
> And gold to the pocket

The bay tree is considered sacred to the earth mother.

BEE ProPolis, Bee Pollen, Bee Jelly All products of the Honey Bee, these various products all have their uses in healing. Bee Propolis is used to bring people back to a sense of reality, being a mental curative agent when used over time. Bee Pollen is a physical curative agent, and may be safely given to anyone who is physically debilitated. Bee Jelly, or 'Royal Jelly,' is a very nutritive food and a strong general tonic to both the human or animal system.

24

B

BEND OVER POWDER   A powder, which is supposed to make other people do your bidding. It is a controlling material that is supposed to be able to control both people and spirits. I would not count on being able to control spirits with any powder.   However, High John the Conqueror, Cubeb Berry powder, or Devil's shoestring powders will control people if prayed over sincerely for what you want them to do.

BELLADONNA   (Atropa Belladonna)   [#327]   Deadly Nightshade   The plant is a narcotic, with sedative, anti spasmodic, and relaxant properties.   It was one of the ingredients in the witches "flying ointment' of the middle ages. It is used in negative magic, but is fortunately difficult to obtain.

BENZOIN {Usually Benzoin of Sumatra}   (Styrax Benzoin) [#2242]   A very powerful incense that raises one closer to the astral planes. It has a spiritualizing effect on people. Calms the place where it is burned, and is a very strong astral purifier. Frequently used to break curses and hexes. A good infumation for the un-evolved, and protective to the evolved.

BERGAMOT   (Mentha Citrata)   [#1473]   Bergamot Mint Used as Melissa Officinalis, Balm, [#1464] (Bergamoto)   Very protective, it adds power to other ritual work, when used in the course of a ritual. Protective in daily life for the person wearing it. An ingredient in many pomades and hair care products.

WILD BERGAMOT   Monarda Fiustulosa   [#1513 or 1514], has a different reputation. The leaves of this plant are used in negative work, mostly for hexing and laying curses.

BETH ROOT   [Trillium Pendulum]   [#2337]   Bethroot is Another supposed love potent, when the powder of the root is added to food. Also known as Southern John, the root is also carried to attract love. It's Latin binomial reveals it use as the bob on dousing pendulums. It is also known as birth root.

BETONY   (Betonica Officinalis)   [#371]   Wood Betony Medically, the root is used as an emetic, to promote vomiting. Magically, it may be used to ward off evil and destroy curses.

25

Supposedly strengthens the body when worn as an amulet. Jupiter and Aries rule it.

The leaves may be made into a light laxative and tonic cordial. They may also be used as an incense, which has slight but useful hex breaking properties.

BETTER BUSINESS INCENSE (Mejor Negocio)   A blend of Cinnamon and Benzoin that is burned to draw money to a place.   It should be used sparingly, once a month is quite enough. Over use destroys its effect.

BILBERRY (Vaccinium Frondosum)   [#2376]   The fruit is used to strengthen the eyesight in those who have difficulties with foggy vision and eyestrain.   Bilberry strengthens the capillaries that feed the eyes, thus restoring, or improving, the functions of the eyes.

Long-term use, over a year, will assist this herb in strengthening all of the body's minor capillaries, and thus gain an over all improvement in skin tone and texture. However, it is primarily used for eyestrain.

Mixed with Thyme, it is used to make a love tea that is said to inflame those who drink it. The leaves, not the berries, are used in making the tea.

BIRCH Bark and Leaves of the tree   (Betula Alba)   [#372] {Betula Alba (folia)} (Abedul)   The bark and leaves are an astringent. The oil is a fragrant addition to massage oils, and may be used as an incense on its own. The gum resin of birch is a useful incense that has found a number of uses among Native American Indian practitioners. There is a birch essential oil available.

BIRTHWORT   (Aristolochia Longa)   [#249]   Long Birthwort   Related to (A. Serpentaria   Virginia Snakeroot #253) The root is used to remove obstructions after childbirth.

BISTORT   [Polygonum Bistorta]   [#1784]   The root is carried as a charm, or burned as an incense. Used to attract wealth to a place or to a person.   It must be dried and powdered before being burned. It is considered to be a herb of psychic power, as it removes obstructions to material prosperity from the place where it is burned. It is ruled by Saturn. Medically, it is used as a gargle and mouthwash.

BITTERSWEET [Solanum Dulcamara] [#2178] Root and Twigs Another member of the nightshade family that is used in both protection and cursing. Mercury rules the herb.

The twig is used in palo magic, as bitterwood, in contrast to the sweet wood of Licorice. Bittersweet root is also said to be a strong aphrodisiac if used sparingly. (No more than once a day, preferably less often.)

Medically, it was once used in the treatment of venereal disease, where it was eventually found to be ineffective. The root may be carried as a charm for protection against evil.

The root is also used to return or place curses. A handful of this root is placed in the hand, and the following, or a similar, curse is pronounced on the person. When the verbal curse is completed, the herb is cast in the direction of the one to be cursed.

"Oh Lucifer, plague my enemy ___N. N.___ with all of your powers. Curse his heart to ache, his body to burn with pain, his words to turn to bitter gall, and his feet to turn from his intended path."

BLACK ART (Arte Negro) Oil, Incense, Powder Used in spells of destructive negative magic, and in laying curses. It can be dangerous to the user if you are not very careful in using it. The incense must be only be used out of doors. These products are primarily made of crab shell powder, cattail candle powder, with some sulfur, and usually some asafetida added. The oil base used for negative magic is either mineral oil, lard, or tallow. The incense may have an expediter added to it, but do not use any of the mercury compounds. Wash your hands after working with this product, and then rinse them with holy water you have previously consecrated. This work may rebound on you if you are not careful as you do it. Always write out the prayer you will use with this kind of work in advance.

To hex a person, write their name thirteen times on a piece of scrap paper. This is a piece of paper that would otherwise be thrown out, such as a paper grocery bag, or paper wrappings of some kind. Place magically charged black art powder over the names, and fold the paper to make a packet, folding away from you each time. Now sprinkle some powdered sulfur over the packet, and once again make the prayer of the curse over it. Then take the packet to a cemetery, where you must toss the packet over the fence in the direction of a fresh grave, as you pronounce aloud again the curse that you wish to lay on the person.

BLACK CANDLE TOBACCO   Made from a tobacco twist or hand of black, or at least a very strong dark, tobacco. The tobacco is mixed with an equal amount of sea salt and burned on charcoal after lighting a black candle.

The spell using this incense is one used to win court cases, and to overcome legal entanglements. It may also be used to curse lawyers and judges.

BLACK CAT POWDER The occult store version is usually powdered willow or pine wood flour, colored black with soot. It may best be made from ebony wood powder. That powder may be prayed over and used as a casting powder, to take the luck away from someone, having an effect like a black cat crossing their path. It gives the victim a minor hex.

BLACK CAT POWDER   A powder used to attract the opposite sex for sexual purposes. The powder is rubbed on the genitals of the person who desires sexual contact. This powder is made as follows:

> Five or six hairs from a female black cat in heat
> A pinch of iron fillings
> A bay leaf
> A pinch of ground myrrh powder

Grind together in the mortar until thoroughly mixed. The quantity made is usually small. Enough is made at one time for a single application.

B

When the powder is made for or by a man, the hairs should be taken from a black tomcat in heat.

BLACK CHICKEN (Gallina Negra)   A jinx removing product whose name is taken from a jinx removing or spiritual cleansing ritual.   The ritual involves a fan made from black chicken feathers, or on occasion a black chicken, which is used to clear negativity from a person.   The spiritual cleansing ritual works far better than any powder or oil.

BLACK COHOSH ROOT (Cimicifuga Racemosa) [#616] Used primarily for women, Black Cohosh is said to be useful in alleviating menstrual difficulties and similar female complaints.

This herb will supply a natural form of estrogen, and thus combat hot flashes and other problems of menopause. It also will assist in maintaining proper blood pressure, although it is more useful for women in this regard than for men. A mild relaxant to the system. Used in a bath it is said to be protective to women. Magically, the root is boiled in water, the water is then used as a purifying sprinkle in the home.

BLACK DEVIL POWDER   Wheat flour, and a green powdered colorant, with a bit of sugar and salt from the table. This powder is prayed over and sprinkled on the undergarments of the spouse to keep them from disporting themselves sexually with someone else.

BLACK DEVIL POWDER This version of the powder is used to force a wayward lover to give up their extra marital sexual interests. The powder is mixed with an equal quantity of confectioners sugar and placed on the underwear of the straying partner. This powder should be used in conjunction with Orange Powder and prayer to restore the sexual nature of the relationship. It is made as follows:

> Dried Gardenia petals and leaves ½ Ounce
> Orris Root Powder – ½ Ounce
> Cinnamon Powder – ¼ Ounce
> Ground Bay Leaf 1/4 Ounce

Mix together grinding to a find mesh. Sift several times to get a good blend. Bottle and let it digest a week or two. To use, take about a quarter teaspoon of the powder and place on the underwear of the unfaithful spouse.

BLACK HAW TREE   (Viburnum Prumifolium) [#2422] The leaves are used as a tea, the bark of the root as a tonic. The powder of the root bark is also used as a casting powder, with indifferent results.

BLACK MUSTARD SEED [#2157] Used like Peony Seeds or Jumby Beans, to cause disturbances and problems in a place. It is prayed over and cast on the floor in the place to be troubled. See Mustard.

BLACK POWDER   (Polvo Negro)   Made from ebony wood powder. In some cases, carbon black is added to make it even darker. The material is used as an incense and in an oil, both to lay curses and to remove them. It acts as a booster to other cursing materials, but may also be used to remove curses from other people.   Straight ebony powder will work as well as anything else for curse breaking.

BLACK WALNUT   (Juglans Nigra) [#1252] See Walnut The Bark is used as an astringent, and to stop hexes. The tea, made from the nut, is an effective potent for cleansing the astral body of the after effects of a sexual relationship.   It provides both a cleansing effect and a separating effect.

BLACK WILLOW   (Salix Nigra) [#2014] Pussy Willow The bark is used to make a bitter tea used in love spells as a casting liquid. The catkins, or buds, are used in love charms. A bush of the New Moon, it has a bad reputation aside from its use in negative and controlling magic.

BLACKBERRY   Leaves and Root (Rubus Villosus) [#1979] The bark of the root is used in dysentery, as is the wine. The powder of the peelings from the bark is made into a sweeping powder to keep money in the house.

B

BLADDERWRACK (Fucus Versiculosus) [#1017]   Carried for protection while traveling, especially while traveling by water.   It is often used to give someone a bladder or urinary infection.   The powder is prayed over, and a mound of it, say at least a quarter teaspoon, is put near a toilet they regularly use. This spell is said to take about two months to cause the victim to develop symptoms of a urinary infection.   It is also said to be able to cause mental derangement in a person.

Known as Sea Wrack, it yields Kelp, a treatment in obesity.

BLESSED OIL   Used to anoint people following a spiritual cleansing, or at any other time.   Made from Lotus root powder, Orris root powder and Olive oil. Let it stand for a while before use.

BLESSED POWDER   Sprinkled around a room to cleanse and purify it.   This powder may be rubbed on the body for spiritual cleansing and carried in a charm bag for protection. Made from Lotus root flour, it makes an excellent cleansing medium when used by a spiritual worker for that purpose.   It may be given to the people to use on themselves, in which case it should be diluted half and half with talc.

BLESSED POWDER   Another blessed powder is a purifying agent.   It is sprinkled around a room, on a person, or on an object to purify and protect.   It is used to attract beneficial spiritual influences to a person, place, or thing.   It may be used to assist qa person in walking a more pure path, by placing a pinch of the powder in their shoes.   It is not a curse breaker, or an uncrossing powder.   It may be placed in the corners of a room, or sprinkled on the floor of the room.   It should be prayed over before use, using the name of the person to be helped.   It is made as follows:

>Blessed Thistle Herb – 1 ounce
>Fenugreek - ¼ ounce
>Orris Root Powder - ½ ounce
>Magnesium Carbonate - ¼ Ounce

Mix well and sift several times to a consistent fineness.   It may blown on the person or rubbed on the spinal column or the back of the neck.

BLESSING POWDER (Benediction Powder) One of the best powders that may be used for blessing others is made from one third Orris root flour and two thirds Lotus root flour. This is an entirely herbal powder, and it should not be thinned out or diluted with anything. This blessing powder may be used for blessing a person after a spiritual cleansing, or used at any other time a blessing powder may be required. It is a very handy powder for many blessing and cleansing applications in everyday magical and spiritual use.

One example of the use of this powder is in uncrossing either yourself or another person, by making three equal limbed crosses on the chest with the blessing powder. This is followed by making a cross on the forehead, after which you should place your hands on the head of the person being blessed and pray over them that they may be uncrossed and blessed.

Blessing powder used to un-hex or purify a room may be made from 100% Lotus root flour. It is sprinkled around the room, to purify it after the room has been spiritually cleansed. It may also be rubbed on the body of a person while praying for their elevation and spiritual protection.

BLESSED THISTLE [Centaurea Benedicta] [#558] Used primarily as a good luck charm, it adsorbs negativity, although it usually has taken in its quota of negativity in a few days, or a week's, time. Used medicinally as an appetite stimulant, or as a general tonic.

BLESSING (Bendicion) Oil See above.

BLOOD INKS These are the inks theoretically used to write pacts with the devil, draw magical sigils, and for other magical purposes. I prefer Higgins drawing inks, as they have more colors available, and look nicer when the sigil is done. However, if you are into blood, you must recognize that blood congeals quite fast, and if left out, it will draw flies. The best arti coagulant I know of is citric acid, known as sour salt, and available in the Kosher Foods section of your super market.

B

Make up a saturated solution of citric acid with water. Add about three drops of the solution to every teaspoon of blood you are using. Stir it in, you may need to add more, watch the ink to be certain that to does not coagulate as you write out your pact or sigil.

Doves blood ink is best made from ripe poke berries. This makes a very long lasting ink, although it turns a kind of blood brown with age. Do not write on enamel coated paper with this ink, use parchment, ordinary paper, or papyrus.

You can also make a satisfactory blood ink from 'Blood Meal,' a fertilizer product found in your local garden supply store. Make up about a tablespoon of blood meal to a tablespoon of water, and thin to suit. This is probably the most effective way to make and use blood inks, and also the least destructive to your happy household.

BLOOD ROOT (Sanguinaria Canadensis) [#2041] Used to defeat hexes and spells. It is carried on the person in a red charm bag. It is put on windows or doorways to protect against curses and evil spirits. It may also be burned as an incense once a week. It becomes useless if burned more frequently.

As a protective, the powdered bloodroot is cast on the door of the dwelling of someone who you believe is working against you. It turns their spells back against them if it is prayed over for this purpose.

Used medically for coughs due to colds. A tonic and emetic.

Another more rare use is to make Diabolic Wine, a substitute for human blood in rituals of demonism or of a diabolic nature. A pinch of powdered blood root is added to any dark red wine, and mixed in well. The wine is then left overnight covered, with a red cloth. Before using, the wine is changed to blood, by praying the following over it three times, while charging it.

"You are not wine but blood. Living Blood, Scarlet Blood, Living Blood, flowing blood of Mine."

The ritual is then proceeded with, using the wine in place of any required animal or other blood.

BLUEBERRY LEAVES   (Vaccinium Frondosum)   [#2376] The powder is said to cause strife and confusion when tossed in the path, or at the doorway, of an enemy. A cold overnight soaking tea of the leaves is also used for laying curses. It is a casting liquid, poured out across the doorway of the enemy at night.

BLUE COHOSH   (Caulophyllum Thalictroides)   [#545] {Calouphyllum Thalic Troid}   The root is used medicinally, and in root working. The root is also known as Yellow ginseng, and is worked for healing spells as well.

BLUESTONE Incense, Crystals, Copper Sulfate, also known as Blue Crystal, and Blue Vitrol, (CuSO4) It has formerly had wide uses in magic, as it is the primary ingredient of the famous Wound Salve and the Weapon Salve, as well as of the Bandage Heal All spell. As a crystal, it has been used as an ingredient in love spells, as it draws the desire nature. (Copper the metal of Venus rules the desire nature, the Sulfate of any Metal draws things of the nature of the metal).

However, this toxic substance can cause liver damage, eye and skin problems, and even death. Corrosive to the skin, it is not ever recommended for use. The ingestion of either the product or the fumes from burning it can easily prove fatal. It has a very nasty action on the kidneys, which can result in either a slow, and quite painful kidney failure, or a slow and painful death. This is why no formula is given for making this material. Don't use it for anything. The penalty is not worth the risk you will be taking.

Despite the possibility of its causing all kinds of physical illnesses, it is a favorite powder in love and sex magic. For many years, it was used by professional women in the south, particularly in New Orleans, for attracting customers. Burning the crystals as incense produces hazardous toxic fumes, and is never recommended. I do not recommend that it ever be used, despite its long history of successful application.

B

BOLDO LEAVES (Pemis Boldus) [# none] The dried and crushed leaves are used in power spells. Whether or not they actually add any power to the spell is always open to question.

BONESET (Eupatorium Perfolaitum) [#962] Used to curse enemies with accidents resulting in broken bones. It is burned as an incense while the following spell is chanted:

> I alone can break your bones,
> You may no longer harm me.
> Now the harm you do
> Will return to you.
> So Be It!

Medically, boneset has been used in the past in the form of a poultice, or as a plaster, to heal broken bones.

BORAGE Tops (Borago Officinalis) [#402] The plant has medicinal uses. The tea made from the tops of the plant is given to young boys to develop courage in them. Thus, Borage for Courage.

BOSS FIX POWDER This powder is used to reduce threats to employment, and to reduce or eliminate difficulties on the job. It is to be sprinkled around the work place to improve the conditions of the work environment. This powder should be used in conjunction with cinnamon protection powder, as well as any other work that may be necessary in the specific circumstance. Often achieving a satisfactory resolution to work related problems may require a great deal of work, both on the work site and on the person involved.

Boss Fox powder is made from ground toasted Indian corn, and ground white eggshell. The two should be ground together into a fine powder in the mortar. The ground powder should sit for at least a week before being given to the person to use at their work site. The powder is used by scattering it on the floor around the person's work place.

BOSS FIX POWDER   Another version is used to put an end to harassment on the job, it is sprinkled around the place where the person doing the harassing stands or sits. (It does not have to be the boss or supervisor.)

The powder is simple and effective in its action, and takes a charge well.   It is a powder of Mars, so it must be used carefully, and it's power respected.   If the fault is with the person, rather than the one they are accusing, it is likely that the powder may rebound on the person using it.   Only about a half a teaspoon is needed at any one time.   When only a small amount is used, the person will not usually realize they are being worked against.

> Ground tobacco - 2 ounces
> Ground Chile Powder – 1 ounce
> Iron filings – ½ ounce

Mix the ingredients together and let stand about a week or so before using.   The amount to be used should be prayed over in the name of the person who is being harassed, asking for relief from their harassment.

BRIMSTONE   Best known for its use in negative magic Brimstone is actually hard natural sulfur ore.   It is almost a rock like substance, but quite brittle.   It's color, fresh from the mine, is a dark and impure looking yellow.   Refined Flowers of Sulfur Powder has a bright yellow color.   Except for the most critical magical work, they may be substituted one for the other.

BROOM   (Cytisus Scoparius)   [#834]   Broom tops, or Broom herb is an astral cleansing agent that removes negativity wherever it is applied.   It is usually used as a tea to wash things, or as a sprinkle, to clear a home, or other area.   It may also be used in a cleansing spiritual bath, where it is very effective indeed.   The Broom plant is often referred to as the astral broom.

BROOM TOPS -   Broom tops from the European broom plant, are used to make up a cleansing solution known as the 'astral broom.'   The solution is made by soaking a hand full of broom tops in alcohol (extracted from Vodka) in the refrigerator for a week or so.   Another handful of broom tops are steeped in

B

boiling water until the water reaches room temperature. They are then both placed in the refrigerator for another week or so and the two are mixed together. A cup of this mixture in a gallon pail of water is the bathing solution. It is poured slowly over the person's head as they stand in a tub or shower. The newly cleaned person should air dry and dress in clean clothing.

BRUNO'S CURSE (Maldicion De Bruno) See Knot Weed

BUCHU Leaves (Barosma Crenulata (or Crenata)) [#351] Used in making a Spring Tonic.

BUCKEYE NUT (Horse Chestnut) (Aesculus Hippocastanum) [#75] (Castano) Often carried as a charm against arthritis and rheumatism. It can adsorb some of the pain of these afflictions from the person, as it accepts the pain vibration into the nut. Once the shell of the nut breaks however, it is overloaded and should be discarded. A salve made from it is also used for hemorrhoids. See Chestnut.

Incense is made from the nut as well. The skin of the horse chestnut is peeled off first, and the nuts are dried and then crushed. Then they are more fully dried, and powdered. The incense is burned both for luck and to send back an illness or a curse. Use infrequently, as it is easily over used.

BRYONY (Bryony Alba) [#420] White Bryony Said to have been one of the primary healing herbs of the Rosicrucian's. The root and berries are used medicinally, although they are considered toxic. The medicinal qualities are extracted by water or alcohol. Ruled by Mars, the peelings of the outer covering of the root are used as an incense in work done for Mars.

BUGLEWEED Lycopus Virginicus [#1411] It is a sedative, and a mild narcotic. Good for relief from a cough. This plant takes a magical charge well. The dried flowers make a delicate incense of Venus.

BURNING BUSH   (Euonymus Atropurpureus)   [#950]
Wahoo   The seeds are a cathartic.   The bark of the tree is the famous Wahoo Bark, used for removing malochia and minor hexes.   The bark of the root is also used in a bath for this purpose.

BURDOCK ROOT   (Articium Majus (or Lappa)) [#237]
The plant is used in medicine, the seeds are crushed and used in incense.

BUTTON SNAKE ROOT   (Erynigium Yuccifolium)   [#931]
The corn snake root.   Also see Liatris Spicata, [#1338]   The true button Snakeroot, which is used in treating Bright's disease.   The herb is added to spells for faster work, but it is not a very good expediter.

C

CACTUS FLOWERS   (Cactus Grandiflowers)   [#437]
Night Blooming Cereus, which see.

CALABAR BEANS   (Physostigma Venosum)   [#1712]
Ordeal bean   The beans are **poison**, death occurring within an hour. Used as a sedative, as it depresses the central nervous system, thus used medically in epilepsy. Magically, the beans are used in the ritual of Suestro. This is known as the "Theft of the Soul," which it is not. It is a ritual for putting someone under the control of the magician.

CALAMUS (Acorus Calamus) [#60] Sweet Flag Used as a protective herb, especially in conjunction with other herbs.

Baths, sprays, and sprinkles, may be made of it alone. A broom made of Calamus herb may be used in cleansing of people. This is the "sweet cane broom," used in brushing negativity from people and places, in some of the full formal spiritual cleansings used to sweeten their lives. The tea is a remedy for upset stomach.

CALENDULA (Calendula Officinalis) See Marigold.

CAMOMILE [Anthemis Nobilis] [#205] {Matricaria Chamomilla} The flowers, in tea form, make a nervine, as well as a strong astral condenser, or an astral strengthener. The extract and sucess are used to strengthen the astral body and promote healing of wounds.

Used in warm compresses of a strong tea, and placed on the damaged skin, it promotes healing of the skin. Useful in cases of wrinkled skin, wind burned and sun exposed skin, and overly dry skin. The tea helps regulate the menses. Ruled by the Sun and Mercury.

Using the tea as a hand wash before gambling is a common practice.

ROMAN CHAMOMILE Anthemis Nobilis, is more difficult to obtain.

CAMPHOR Gum [Laurus Camphora] [#1302] Used to gain prophetic dreams, to clear a ritual area, and for other purposes. It may be burned as an incense for these purposes. Natural gum camphor is one of the oldest incenses used by mankind. The leaves of the camphor tree are ruled by the Yoruba deities Chango and Eshu, thus they make an excellent bath for young pre pubescent boys.

CANADA SNAKE ROOT (Asarum Canadenese) [#280] Wild Ginger The root is used to relieve stomach disorders. It is used in incenses, to induce visions, and in love potions.

CANDLE OIL The generic name for oil, or occasionally a powder, used to dress or prepare candles used in magical work. There is no special candle oil, unless it is kerosene or paraffin oil, which was used many years go in the so-called plumbers cardle, an eighteenth and nineteenth century predecessor to the flashlight.

CARAWAY SEED (Carum Carui) [#510] Carried for protection, and used in some magical work, it is not as effective as some other plants. The aromatic and fragrant seeds are useful as an incense, having a cleansing effect when burned on charcoal. Some of the seeds sewn into a small white pillow and

40

C

sewn under the child's crib or bed are used to protect children against illness.

CARDAMOM Seed (Ellettaria Cardamomum) [#901] As an incense it has a calming effect on the place where it is burned. It is little used in baths, as it does not have much staying power when used with water.

Occasionally used as a love charm, it is powdered and prayed over, and then added to the beloved's food or drink. In Arabic countries crushed cardamom seed is used to flavor coffee. Medically it is a stomachic. Both the leaves and seeds are used for flavoring sauces, salads, meats, and curries.

CARNATION (Clavel) Oil and Perfume. The perfume is made from the essential oil. This is a healing scent, which should be worn by nurses, health care, hospital, and nursing home workers. This scent is very protective of people, keeping them from illness. It is a good scent to wear while visiting the sick. A dozen white carnations are a good thing to have in the sick room. White carnations are usually the preferred flowers to use in floral spiritual cleansings.

CASCARA SAGRANDA Buds and Bark [Rhamnus Pur schiana] [#1921] Known as Sacred Bark, it is a bitter tonic. Generally used as a laxative, it has a good effect for this purpose.

In magical work it can be used in a bath to assist in losing weight. A tea is added to the bath water and the individual soaks in it for eight minutes praying that they lose weight. The tea is also said to be effective in winning court cases. In this case, the tea and sprinkled around the living quarters of the person accused, particularly their sleeping area, before they go to court.

CASCARILLA BARK {Croton Eleuteria} [#778] The bark is a medicinal, and used in making Pembas in many of the African origin magico-religious practices.

CASSIA [Laurus Cassia] [#1304] Bastard Cassia Saigon Cassia Cinnamomum Zeylanicum [#639] True Ceylon Cinnamon One of the spices mentioned in the Bible, along with Cinnamon as constituents of the holy incense to be burned before the Lord God. The American Food and Drug Administration classes Cinnamon and Cassia as the same substance, disagreeing with the word of God as given in the Old Testament. As a result, most of the Cinnamon found in stores in the United States is actually Cassia, which is considerably less expensive.

CINNAMOMUM AROMATICUM, [#634] known as Chinese Cinnamon, or Chinese Cassia, is what is most often supplied. It is a variety of Cinnamomum Zeylanicum [#639], however it may not be used to make up the Bible incense, which is only made from Nickles' # 1304 and # 639.

See Cinnamon for the uses of this spice, which has a great many uses in magical practice.

CAT'S CLAW Bark (Uncaria Tomentosa) [NOT # 876] Used as an All Heal, it has a good reputation for assisting in the healing of most human ills. It is especially useful for treating tumors, cysts, and some cancers, which it alleviates rapidly. The powder of the inner bark is used as a dietary supplement for this purpose on a daily basis. It is the herbalist's answer to some surgery.

CATNIP (Nepeta Cataria) [#1575] A calmative and aromatic, it is good for the nerves and stomach. Medically it causes sweats and eases pain. A mild relaxant, it is a halucinogen, especially when used with tobacco. The tea is often used as a curse breaker, for this use it should be sweetened with honey, not with sugar. It may also be used in a love charm, and for feminizing overly masculine women.

CAYENNE PEPPER [Capsicum Annuum] [#492] (Chile, Pimenton) (Capsicum frutescens L.) The world's most popular spice, it is a true stimulant and the most pure Mars herb there is. Used for stomach and circulation problems. It should

C

replace black pepper on the table if you desire to improve your digestion, and aid your general stomach and intestinal function.

The tea is useful for those who have stomach difficulties, but when beginning to use it, the tea must be made very mild, using less than an eighth teaspoon of Cayenne pepper to a quart of water. Those who enjoy spicier foods can gradually increase this dose to their taste. Stimulates the peripheral circulation. It is a primary healing agent for those who know how best to use it.

This pepper is rated in heat units. 90,000 heat units is a typical rating.

Magically, it is used whenever the Martial influence of the 'Act Now' variety is required. It is especially used in works of disruption, hate, and revenge. Always adds heat to any situation. Best used in negative work, but also widely used in works of love and sexual passion.

CEDAR (Cedro) Wood Powder or Oil The material is primarily used for fumigating, to remove negative elementals and to strengthen positive elementals. Cedar sawdust to be used as an incense should have two or three drops of cedar oil added per cup full to strengthen it.

CEDAR OF LEBANON (Cedro de Libano) Oil and perfume. This oil is very similar to regular cedar wood oil as far as I can tell. The technical grade cedar wood oil is sufficiently pure for all magical work. Cedar of Lebanon is also the name of a particular protective spell.

CEDRON SEED (Simaba Cedron) [#2150] Another general tonic. Of the "Spring Tonic" class.

CELERY SEED (Apium Graveolens) [#215] (Apio) A minor calmative, that acts directly on the astral body to remove stuck or difficult emotional forces.

In herbal healing, celery seed is always used in conjunction with another herb, as celery seed loosens the emotional detritus, but does not remove it. It is a good tonic for the liver and also aids in urinary problems. The roots, and large quantities of the seed, are poisonous.

In magic it is used in spells, baths, charms, and incenses, as an expediter, promoting the rapid operation of the work. It is not as fast an expediter as some others, (The toxic red mercuric oxide is probably the fastest working expediter.) but celery seed does work well when used with herbal spells.

Celery Seed is not very good as incense at all, when burned alone it is good in assisting concentration. Otherwise it should be burned with another, more specific, incense and some ground Orris Root to promote astral communication. In this case it expands the specific other incense, and increases its action. Celery seed is ruled by Mercury, but seems to respond to water and earth considerably better than to air and fire. Better used for positive than for negative work.

CELIANDINE (Chelidonium Majus) [#586] The plant was little used in medicine, and probably less used in magic.

CENTAURY (Sabbatia Angularis) [#2001] American Centaury - Medically used as a tonic, it is also used as an eyewash to assist in gaining the astral sight.

CHAMOMILE Roman Camomile [Anthemis Nobilis] [#205] Ruled by the Sun in Leo, it is the emblem of sweetness and humility. Primarily a calmative, Chamomile strengthens the astral (non-physical) body, and assists in strengthening the connection between the astral and mental bodies. A strong tea in a bath is a good treatment for sunburn.

A mild nervine, it is an excellent before bedtime tea, as it prepares the body for sleep. It is often used in love spells, to enhance the astral force projected into it by the lover. As it can go both ways, it may be used to break pride in people. The wash, and a bath of the tea are often used as a gamblers charm. Used in gambling charms and other good luck spells as well, for much the same purpose.

Chamomile is one of the best materials known for adsorbing and holding the astral force. Chamomile tea, made from the whole plant, is one of the best astral condensers that there is.

C

As a general tonic for the body, a solution may be used to treat bites, burns, skin abrasions, and so forth. The material takes a magical charge, or a prayer, very well indeed.

Chamomile success, compounded of the flowers of the plant, mashed, and steeped with pure ethyl alcohol, is used in making magic mirrors as well as enhancing the astral nature of other things. This is one of the reasons it finds such use in magical work.

CHAPPARAL Leaves {Also Creosote plant (Larrea Mexicana [#1294] The plant is an antiseptic. The flowering tops are used as a tonic tea, to improve and maintain good health. In some cases a tea made from the plant is useful for treating cancers.

CHARCOAL, From Vegetable Sources [NONE] Used to draw impurities out of the system. Charcoal capsules and tablets are available, but raw wood charcoal powder may be used for this purpose as well. Charcoal and ashes are infrequently combined for this purpose, but I have never learned what the ashes are supposed to do that the charcoal does not actually do.

CHASE AWAY POWDER Used to remove jinxes and curses, this powder is finely powdered Mate herb, as is used in making Mate tea. This powder is usually used in the course of a full spiritual cleansing, and should be blown on the person from the hand of the person doing the cleansing.

For getting rid of people, see Four Thieves Vinegar or Goofer Dust.

CHERRY Blossoms [# ?] (Cerezo) A bath for increasing self confidence in people is made from these lovely but ephemeral flowers. The bark of the tree is another toxin that is occasionally used in healing. The essential Oil of Cherry usually comes from artificial sources, but it does have a nice scent.

CHESTNUT See Buckeye Nut [#75] The horse chestnut. The nuts are a narcotic.

CHEWING JOHN [?]   The root is chewed and cast away to remove hexes or minor curses from a person. In powdered form, it may be burned as an incense for this same purpose.

Used in money drawing charms, it is placed in a chamois charm bag with three silver coins and prayed over to open opportunities for money to come to you. The charm bag should be carried on the person for at least a month, during which time opportunities will come to the wearer, who must be alert to take advantage of them.

The powdered root is one of the best commanding or compelling powders there is, as it inclines people to have sex with the one who places it on their body. It works in other areas as well, but its use in commanding sexual contact is where it is outstanding.

CHIA   Seed   (Salvia Hispanica)   [#2027]   Used in treating diseases of the eye, it maybe used magically against people to harm their vision.

CHICKWEED (Stellaria Media) [#2225] Used to relieve hives, and other skin rashes. Can be used in a bath for those who have skin problems that are manifesting as excessive itching. The fresh herb is a very healthy addition to green salads. It is also a general tonic for the immune system, especially when taken daily. It assists in preventing colds and other minor illnesses.

CHICORY (Cichorium Intybus) Succory [#612]   The leaves are burned as an incense when ritually casting hexes. The herb is often mixed with coffee, or used alone as a beverage, particularly in the southern U.S. The ground herb is used in laying curses, both as an incense and as a casting powder. Its best magical use is as incense.

CHILD SAINTS   In the Roman Catholic Church there are any number of Child Saints. Those in various religious and magical practices appeal some of them for assistance.

One of the favorite Child Saints is El Nino de Atocha, supposedly a version of the Infant Jesus who fed six hundred

C

Christian prisoners in Atocha Spain from a single basket of food, coming each night for six months. Those who are imprisoned or who have friends or relatives who are imprisoned appeal to him. He is usually asked to make their burden in prison lighter, and assure that they have an early release.

CHINESE Products of all kinds used by Chinese 'Ghost Workers' or other Chinese occult consultants have been unsuccessfully copied for the Botanica and Occult store market. If you speak Chinese you can obtain the originals in the Chinatowns of large cities. The chances you can use them as successfully as the Chinese Ghost worker are as slight as the chances you speak Chinese, (I don't.)

CHIVES Cebolleta (Allium schoenoprasum L.) The condiment is the flat hollow leaves of the plant. Magically, chives are surprisingly responsive to work. While they are not much used, the leaves have considerable ability as the carrier of a magical charge. The leaves may be used for all kinds of work where a casting powder of herbal origin is sought. They are very good for leading a potential lover into a seduction over the salad course.

CHUPAROSA (Hummingbird) A love and romance oil, and perfume very popular in Mexico. It is made with the body of a Hummingbird placed in the bottle.

CHURCH INCENSE (Inglesia) A commercial incense made by the same manufacturers as those who make the well known Gloria Incense. Useful for general work and especially for devotional work. Like all Incenses used in the Roman Catholic Church, it is 51% frankincense, with other ingredients including Benzoin and Myrrh.

CHYPRE OIL - Oil Of Cypress, somewhat difficult to find.
The pure oil is what is best used. A drop of the oil is rubbed into the hands before gambling. The oil is used to bring luck and financial gain. It is most effective in gambling when your hands come into contact with the gambling materials, as in

dice, cards, and so on.   Chypre is said to be the strongest money drawing oil there is.   It is said that J. P. Morgan, the financier, had a special Oil of Chypre after shave lotion made up for him in a bay rum base by a pharmacist.

Chypre Money Powder is made by adding a few drops of oil of Chypre to about a cup of talc.   The powder must be well mixed, and should be aged for at least a week before use.

CINNAMON   Bark, Powdered or Sticks   [Cinnamomum Zeylanicum] [#639] Ceylon Cinnamon (Canela)   Ruled by Mercury, specifically Mercury conjoined with Jupiter in Pisces. Domain of Yemenya.   Cinnamon is one of the most useful powders in magical work.   It brings good fortune in all areas of life.   It is suitable for use as either a blow powder or a casting powder.   It is used to quiet aggression or turbulence, either in the home or between people.   It may be used as a purification, blessing, or protection powder.   Its daily use discourages aggression or negative feelings from others being accepted within oneself.   It may be placed on the forehead, to calm an ill person, or block the fears of well-wishers visiting the ill from harming the sick person.

Widely used in cooking, it is also used in stomach disorders. Said to be an aphrodisiac for women, the tea expels gas and reduces nausea.   It is good to alleviate mild cases of Type 2 diabetes, but see your physician about this.

Often used as a love potion in a tea.   Burned before a voodoo ceremony to make the room sacred.   It has been used for purification, protection, blessing, and prosperity as well. Magically it imparts a mercurial influence in incense mixtures.   It is used to change a person's luck, to improve communications, and to calm a restless nature.

It may be used as incense, in a bath, in powders, oils, or as a sprinkle, or a wash.   The bath is used to help resolve problems, stop quarrels or dissension.   It may also be used to improve income, all depending on the prayer made over the tea.   A dab of cinnamon placed on the breast bone (Sternum) in the morning will keep you protected from envy and jealousy all through your workday.

48

C

The money Cinnamon Bath is made of one cup of Cinnamon tea to 4 cups of Parsley tea. The teas are mixed and the liquid is divided into five parts. The five parts are then prayed over in the name of the person who the baths are to assist. The person must take the five baths on five separate days, praying for financial improvement while in the tub. They are to immerse themselves five to seven times, and stay in the tub for six to eight minutes.

Cinnamon is used as extensively in magic as it is in cooking and baking.

CINNAMON PROTECTION POWDER   This powder will protect the wearer against light cases of malochia, as well as any non-specific vibrations of envy and jealousy that the person may draw to them. The powder is recommended for daily wear at work, as that is the place that most of these negative vibrations seem to originate.

Ground pure cinnamon a quarter teaspoon, Talc four ounces by volume.

The two ingredients are placed in a bottle and mixed together well, shaking the bottle for between five to fifteen minutes. A small amount of the cinnamon protection powder is placed on the index finger and applied to the sternum after bathing, but before dressing each morning. Adding a pinch of powdered clove, or a pinch of fine iron powder may increase the utility of this powder. Adding more than a pinch of these will be of no additional benefit, as the only desire of the additive is to strengthen the vibration of the cinnamon. You should avoid using to much of this powder on yourself. A small amount on the sternum will work as well as using so much you smell like a gumdrop.

Another version of the compound of cinnamon powder is useful in making one's life easier as it reduced the stress and strain of accepting the kind of negativity, complaint, and other nonsense that people send to one every day. It is particularly beneficial when used as an adjutant to the daily toilet. Just place a bit on the sternum every morning, and it will keep you reasonably free of the aggression of others all day long.

Ground Ceylon Cinnamon 2 Ounces
Orrisroot powder ground fine ¼ Ounce
Talcum Powder – 1 lb

Mix thoroughly and seal away for a week or two. Then mix again. Use as a cosmetic talcum powder, although as very small smear on the sternum is usually enough.

CINQUEFOIL   [Potentilla Canadensis]   [#1808]   Also known as five finger grass, this herb is used in charms for improving both speech and confidence in people. It is carried in a charm bag for this purpose. It may also be used in a bath, for the same ends. A bath of Cinquefoil is always recommended before going to an employment interview.

Cinquefoil may also be used to make people speak their minds, by writing the name of the person on a piece of paper and placing Cinquefoil over it. The paper is then prayed over for the effect desired. It is an excellent communications stimulator, and may be used for that purpose. However, it may occasionally make people talk too much. Medically, the tea is a good mouthwash, and is also used as a bath in cases of the night sweats.

CLARIFYING POWDER This powder is used to clarify the mind, clearing the thought processes. It is to be applied liberally to the head and the back of the neck. It is a protective powder, but it must be treated with respect. It is also know as Thinker's Powder. A typical formula for this powder is:

Ground Lotus Root Powder - 1 Ounce
Ground Hazelnut Powder - ½ Ounce
Ground Eggshell Powder - ½ Ounce

Mix well in the mortar, and sift several times for a uniform mix. After making the powder, allow it to sit for a week or longer to blend. After a week, it may be diluted with Talcum powder or Arrowroot, by as much as four ounces to the quantity above.

CLARY (Salvia Selarea) [#2033] Clary Sage An aid in promoting menstruation, it should never be taken by pregnant

C

women as it may cause an abortion. It is said to be an aphrodisiac. Ruled by the Moon.

CLEAVER'S HERB   (Galium Aparine) [#1027]   Used in making farmers cheese occasionally. It is a gentle laxative and cools the human physical system in contradiction to red pepper, which heats the system.

Magically, it may be used to cool a romance by making a tea and pouring a cup of the charged solution into the bath water of the amorous one. This is a good bath to use to quiet young love, if it is used before things get out of hand.

CLOVER   [Trifolium _] (Pratense usually supplied) [#2333   2334]   Red clover tea is used as a heart and blood tonic, and infrequently in love spells. White clover (2334) is used to defeat curses, and cleanse people of negativity.

Neither of the clovers are particularly strong in their effect, having about the same power as the four leafed clover to bring luck. As a plant, it is far better for animals than for mankind.

Red Clover is used as a sprinkle to make a house cleaning more potent. The clover blossoms are soaked in apple cider vinegar for seven days, the solution becomes the sprinkle, which is used after the home is cleansed. This sprinkle makes unfamiliar and unwelcome spirits leave the place.

White Clover mixed with Blue Vervain and Broom tops is used as an uncrossing incense in fumigation's.

CLOVES   (Clavos)   [Caryophyllus Aromaticus] [#517] Ruled by the Sun, Jupiter, and Mercury. In the domain of The Yoruba blacksmith deity Ogun, and thus a herb of Mars. Clove tea, as a gargle, is a good mouthwash, it relieves nausea and promotes health of the teeth and gums. The oil is used to relieve toothaches, rheumatism, and muscle cramps. Powdered clove is mixed with powdered chicory and cinquefoil in about equal quantities to make an incense used to increase mediumship.

The whole clove is used in protective spells. Nine whole cloves are used in a charm bag for vitality. The same charm may be made for protection, depending on the prayer made over it. In an incense it sharpens the tone of the other ingredients. A bath of a tea of powdered cloves is very protective. A Pompadour made with whole cloves, placed stem first into an orange, will act protectively and beneficially toward the one who made it and keeps it with their clothing.

An orange whose outer surface was punctured and filled with whole cloves is considered a good present for a pubescent girl. It is to be kept with her under things to assist in bringing her a suitable marriage partner.

In Indonesia spiritual cleansings are often performed by blowing the smoke of clove cigarettes on the body of the person being cleaned.

CLUB MOSS (Lycopodium Selago) [#1406] Fir The Club Moss Plant was one of the Sacred herbs of the Druids. This herb was supposedly picked by someone who had been specially purified. A herb of purification. The powder of the spores is used as a flash powder for dramatic effects in rituals.

COCONUT (Coco) The oil and milk of the coconut both have a place in magical work. Used in feeding the head, (Eleda) the milk of the coconut may be purchased at Asian stores. Powdered coconut is also available, it may be used to stop negative magic by spreading it around the place where the negative magic is practiced, or where the spell has been laid.

COD LIVER OIL From the codfish, not from a plant source. Used to decrease blood pressure, as well as being used as a laxative. It works to oppose autointoxication, through encouraging regularity of the elimination function. Occasionally used as a base in magical oils.

COFFEE (Coffea Arabica) [#685] (Cafe) There are a variety of uses for coffee in magical practice. The best known is the coffee bath, for strengthening the etheric sheath.

Placing three to six cups of coffee in a tub of water and soaking in it for eight to ten minutes make this bath. An exception to most spiritual baths, you may use soap and bath oil in this bath without diluting the effects of the bath.

C

Liquid coffee may be used to strengthen the non-physical component of anything upon which it is wiped, washed, or soaked. It becomes a good thing to wipe furniture with after washing it with a vibe remover, such as ammonia water, as it can restore the damage that has been done to the furniture's astral and etheric body.

Coffee chaff, the husk of the coffee bean, is used as an incense ingredient in working with invisible forces. It is useful to add some to the myrrh incense used in summoning to visible appearance. Doing so adds stability to the appearance of the shade, which is usually quite unstable.

Fresh ground coffee is used as a body rub to remove long-standing, or even karmic, negativity from people. This must be done carefully, as the person doing it must have the moral authority to remove the negativity.

To solve or resolve problems, place a brief description of the problem in some ground coffee. Hide the package (of coffee and the problem) away in a dark place. In a week or so the problem will disappear.

Aside from the uses of brewed coffee, the perfume and oil, made from the essential oil, are also useful in magic. Coffee powder, the roasted and ground bean, is used magically in the espresso grind and in Turkish coffee, which is even more finely ground. The latter is the best to use in incenses, either used alone, or blended with other ingredients.

COLA NUTS   KOLA NUTS   (Cola Acuminata)   [#687] The Goona Nut, (Source of Goona Goona?)   Used in IFA Divination in Yorubaland, from whence comes the demand for them among followers of the Yoruba Orisha based practices. The nut itself is a stimulant and a nervine.

COLORS   The outside of temples and churches are usually painted white, to reflect any negative influences away from them. Red is said to invigorate the spirits of the dead, so it is often used to paint séance rooms. Black is said to adsorb negative and other non-physical influences.

In addition, there is an entire study of the psychology of colors, dealing with how people react to various colors. This is something often worth studying by those who consult or counsel others. The color of clothing clients wear is often a key to their state of mind.

COLTSFOOT (Tussilago Farfara) [#2348] Good for the relief of coughs, it is ruled by Venus. The leaves are used in a tea.

COMFREY Leaves and Root [Symphytum Officinale] [#2253] Best known for healing broken bones, the root of this herb of Saturn is often used in ointments for healing skin, and for providing relief from itching. A well-known tonic, and cough remedy as well. Medically, it is also used to clear up bloody urine. It is good for wounds, strains, and sprains. The tea is used as a sprinkle to improve business. Used in charm bags for safe journeys. The tea of the root is often used as a charm for protection. The leaves are used to add stability to herbal spells.

COME TO ME POWDER A powder used for sexual attraction. It announces that you are looking for a lover, and draws people to the wearer. You will have to sort out the ones you want however, as this powder does not discriminate, it only draws people to you.

> Ground Orrisroot powder - 1 ounce
> Sweet Pea Oil - 20drops

Mix thoroughly and store in a closed container for a week or more to allow the Orrisroot powder to fully adsorb the Sweet Pea oil. Shake the container every day to encourage mixing. Then add the prepared powder to the following mixture.

> Talcum powder – 4 to 6 Ounces
> Powdered Myrrh – ¼ teaspoon

Sift together several times to make a uniform mixture, and store in a closed container, allowing the mixture to set for a week to digest. To use apply to the sternum and the sides of the neck.

COMMANDING (Dominarte) CONTROLLING (Controlando) COMPELLING (Apremiante) Oils, Powders,

C

Perfumes. The purpose of these products is to allow the person using them to gain control over another person and make them do what the controller wants them to do. There are any numbers of other names for these products, but they all are made with the same end in mind. Ruling Powders, King Maker products, and Bend Over products are a few of these alternative names. There is no really effective incense for this purpose. The powders usually have a herbal base, and occasionally is consist entirely of the herbal material. The products are made from a commanding herb, such as High John the Conqueror, Devil's Shoe String, Cubeb berries, or Calamus Root. The Oil is usually the herb, or the herbal powder in an oil, usually mineral oil. The perfume is usually the powder or herb in a convenient perfume base. The products are usually applied directly to the person to be controlled. The secret to using any of these products is that they must be prayed over individually, for each person to be controlled, and for each use.

COMMANDING POWDER This powder is used to compel another person to do what you desire. It will make the person do what you wish them to do. It is used in dominating another person, especially in a short-term situation.

> Devil's shoestring powder – 1 Ounce
> Hand of Power powder – 1 Ounce
> Orris Root Powder – 1 Ounce

Sift together several times and store for a week or two. To use, take about a quarter teaspoon of the powder and add a drop of whiskey. Pray over the powder and tell it what you want done. With the powder in your hand, cast it in the path of the person, or place a bit of it on them.

To speed the action of the powder, add a pinch of iron filings before it is used.

CONCENTRATION (Concentration) Incense, Oil, Perfume The best incense for this purpose is Alum, which has very little odor at all. Any product with the vibration of Saturn may be used for gaining these ends, whichever is selected, it must be prayed over for the best results. The best oil base for making the oil is mineral oil.

CONCENTRATION POWDER Used to assist developing the powers of concentration, may be used when studying or meditating. To use, place a small amount on the third eye point of the forehead, along with a prayer for increased concentration.

Gum Mastic ½ Ounce
Alum 1/8 Ounce

Mix well in the mortar and store in a closed bottle.

CONDURANGO Bark   (Marsdenia Condurango) [NOT #290]   Eagle Vine. Considered to be a cancer remedy as Condurango Blanco. I would put more faith in my physician than this supposed remedy.

CONFUSION POWDER Made from crab shell powder and peppermint leaf powder. Apply to the person or their trace to confuse their mind. It can be used to make a person mentally dwell on the past, or on an experience in their past, which the magician selects by forming a thought form of the experience during the prayer over the spell.

CONFUSION POWDER A powder used to confuse those working against the user, this may be used prior to any attempt at uncrossing someone. It is also used to discourage someone from prying into the user's affairs.

The powder is a general agent of confusion, as it dulls the mind of the person it is used against. This is a very versatile powder, considering all of its many uses.

Wood ashes 1 Ounce
Cinquefoil Herb ½ Ounce
Jasmine Flower leaves ½ Ounce
Ashes of Peppermint leaves ½ Ounce

Sift together casting out all lumpy matter. Add one drop of Jasmine Oil and One drop of Acacia (Gum Arabic) water. Mix and store in a closed container for a week. Sift again to mix well, add about an ounce of Orrisroot powder, and mix thoroughly once again. Use only about an eighth of a teaspoon

C

at a time, casting in near the person or placing some of it on their person.

CONQUERING GLORY (Conquistar Gloria) Incense Burned in a ritual used to over come obstacles in the path to success. The powder of the ground incense may be sprinkled on the hands and feet of the person each morning for a specific number of days afterwards.

This incense is also used in fumigation's for overcoming timidity. The incense is made of equal parts of Pomegranate bark, cherry bark, and Benzoin, with other herbs added as required in the specific case. When the incense is to be used as a sprinkling or anointing powder, a bit of gold leaf is often added.

CONSECRATION OIL (Fuerza Consagrado) An oil usually used for consecrating ritual instruments, the ritual area, and other things. Ordinary cooking oils, Olive, Canola, Sunflower, etc., are often used for this purpose. The consecration is effected by the prayer made over the oil. Using the oil and powder mixture listed under blessing oil or anointing oil may result in a better oil.

CORAL ROOT (Corallorhiza Odortorhiza) [#731] Crawley Root A sedative useful in releasing nervous tension and cramps. Ruled by the Moon.

CORIANDER Seeds (Culantro) [Coriandrum Sativum] [#739] The plant is ruled by Mars. Another spice used as a love potion. Once again, it is to be prayed over and mixed in with the victim's food or drink. In Arabia, the ground seeds are often added to Coffee as a flavoring agent, and an aphrodisiac. They are also added to wine for the same purpose. The leaves are used in salads and sauces.

A stomach tonic, as well as being beneficial for the heart. The fruit is ruled by Venus, it is used in sachets and incenses. In India it is used as an offering to the deities of the Hindu pantheon. Magically the seeds are an astral stabilizer, and should be used whenever another ingredient in the spell 'goes both ways' to prevent the switching that might otherwise occur.

Those who suffer from migraine headaches carry the seeds in charm bags.

CORN FLOWER (Centaurea Cyanus) [#561] The Blue Centaury The best possible sprinkle for the kitchen of a home. It is a good sprinkle to use both inside and outside of the home as well, as it aids in bringing peace and harmony to a marriage. Keeping cornflowers in the kitchen is said to keep food in the kitchen.

It was the favorite flower of the famous German Chancellor Bismarck, and worn by his followers and supporters as an act of rebellion when the 'Iron Chancellor' was dismissed as first minister of Germany.

CORNSILK (Tassels of Zee Maze) The tea is a specific for urinary and bladder complaints. Two or three cups a day will usually clear up the complaint in a week or two.

CORRESPONDENCE The doctrine of correspondences is the belief that things of one nature have a relationship to things of another nature. Thus the astrological sign Aries corresponds to Red, as they both correspond to the planet Mars, which rules Aries. Some example correspondences follow:

Aries, red, Myrrh, black pepper, ginger
Taurus, green, oak moss, patchouli, & Ylang-Ylang.
Gemini, yellow, lavender, lemongrass, peppermint.
Cancer, blue, Melissa (true lemon balm), chamomile and yarrow.
Leo, orange, frankincense, bay, lime, & neroli.
Virgo, yellow / green, sandalwood, clary sage, and cypress.
Libra, peach, rose, Orris, and vanilla
Scorpio, purple, basil, pennyroyal, and thyme
Sagittarius, burgundy, clove, nutmeg, and hyssop.
Capricorn, forest green, Benzoin, tonka and vetivert.
Aquarius, metallic gold, spikenard, lemon verbena and

C

anise

Pisces, cobalt blue, cardamom, Palma Rosa, and Jasmine.

I would like to thank Mr. Edmond H. Wollmann, a Professional member of the American Federation of Astrologers for providing this useful list.

COTTON ROOT BARK (Algod on) (Gossypium Herbaceum) [#1096] The tea of the bark is used as an abortifacient.

COTTON SEED The tea of the seed in a bath is supposed to attract men to the woman who bathes in it. Formerly it was used in love spells, and by professional women to draw customers. The seeds are also supposed to restore male potency.

COUCH GRASS (Triticum Repens) Witch Grass Dog Grass [#2340] The root is a diuretic and a laxative. The powdered dried root is used as an incense in love rituals.

COUMARIN HERB POWDER [Unknown] One of the Love herbs used in potions, incenses, and sachets.

COURAGE (Valor) Bath, Water To make the weak brave and self confident. The best magical technique for this is the cherry blossom bath, made from a pint of cherry blossoms and a quart of hot water. Steep the cherry blossoms in the water until the water reaches room temperature. Add to bathe and bathe for eight minutes with at least five immersions.

Failing this, or in addition to it, a mouthwash made of cinquefoil tea will at least let the person speak up for himself or herself.

COURT CASE A large number of spells have to do with success in a law court. The kind of people who are best acquainted with these spells may be judged by the fact that most of them are for criminal cases. One for a civil case, used to gain a favorable judgment is to hold seven Guinea peppers in your mouth when you enter the courtroom. Then flick them up near the judge's bench just as your case is called. It inclines the judge to favor your cause.

COURTING POWDER   Used to gain a relationship with another person. It is not a lust powder, nor is it a controlling powder. This powder only breaks down barriers to friendship and personal relationships. A teaspoon of clove and a teaspoon of Allspice added to a cup of talc make the powder. The person using it should apply some to the person whose acquaintance they wish to make, and to their own sternum.

This powder is also useful for salesmen making sales calls. It tends to make people react favorably to them.

Another courting powder, this one a mild love powder used more for gaining acquaintance than having sex. Used to create a desire in another to marry, but for this purpose also see Orange Powder.

Dried pink rose petals - 1 ounce
Orris Root Powder - 4 Ounces

Mix well, sifting together several times. To use, pray over it for what is desired by name.

COWSLIP FLOWERS (Primula Veris) [#1822]   Cowslip Primrose   A tonic, sedative and antispasmodic.

CRAMP BARK   (Viburnum Opulus)   [#2421]   An anti spasmodic, good for all cases of cramps and muscular spasms. Used in crossing rituals to place a hex on someone to variable effect.

CRANBERRY   [Vaccinium Oxycoccos]   [#2378]   The primary dietary treatment for kidney and emotional problems of all kinds. Cranberry juice and sauce are very useful in cleansing the emotional or astral body of emotional blockages.

As a preventative, it is best taken as Cranberry sauce, served with chicken that has been cooked with Tarragon. This gives the Cranberry its best effect, as the Chicken and Tarragon combine to assist in the astral healing process.

C

The extract of Cranberry may be taken whenever there is a severe emotional difficulty to be worked through. However, using too much Cranberry can add Oxalic acid to the system. Thus, caution must be used when adding cranberry to the diet. Use moderation, rather than excess.

CRAWLEY ROOT   (Corallorhiza Odontorhiza)   [#731] Dragon's Claw   It is a diaphoretic and a sedative.   It is excellent in the relief of fevers, cramps and night sweats. (See Coral Root)

CROSSING (Cruzando) Oil, Incense, Powder   Crossing mixtures are used to lay jinxes or curses, or to place people in a crossed condition, where they have difficulties with their life. The cattail head, or candle makes an effective crossing powder, when it is prayed over for the effect desired, using the name of the person it is to affect.

A useful crossing oil may be made of mineral oil and the ground powder of the cattail head. A bit of asafetida may be added to make the oil complete. The oil should be placed on a bit of cotton and prayed over for the person, with the desired curse spoken in the prayer. The oiled part of the cotton is applied to the one who is to be the victim, or placed somewhere they will accept it. The one doing this should avoid touching the oil.

An excellent, but quite dangerous, crossing incense may be made from flowers of sulfur and copper sulfate, ground together in the mortar. The odor is toxic and quite unpleasant and it must be burned out of doors for the best results. The trace of the person may be suspended over this incense as it burns, allowing the trace to be thoroughly fumigated by these toxic fumes. I do not recommend this incense for use, as it is too likely to rebound on the user.

An excellent crossing powder that may be used to cast spells on rivals, on those you wish to harm or destroy. Also, see, Grave Yard Dust, High Conquering Powder, and Wormwood Powder. Use the following as a casting powder, about a quarter teaspoon full at a time. Pray over the powder by name and cast in the path of the person you wish to curse. Use only one application per lunar month.

> Powdered tobacco - 2 Ounces
> Iron Filings - 1 Ounce
> Powdered Basil Herb - ½ Ounce
> Powdered Orris Rout - ½ Ounce
> Talcum Powder - ¼ Ounce

Mix well together sifting several times and store in a dark place for a week or so. The purpose of talc in the above is to assist in the blending of the ingredients. Do not dilute if the best results are desired.

CROWNING GLORY POWDER   A powder used in

overcoming obstacles to success. It is a better practice to use a particular powder more suited to eliminate the specific obstacle perceived in the path.

The following comes from a Haitian Voodoo Mambo:

Take one piece of real gold leaf, put about a teaspoon full of red sanders in it, and cover the red sanders with ground frankincense. Add just a few grains of sea salt, and mix it all up, the gold leaf goes right into the mixture. Put the mixture in a bottle with a Tonka bean that has been soaking in seawater, and leave the mixture in the light of the sun for a week or so. Take it out and make the powder fine again. To use it, make the sign of the cross with it on the hands and feet every day before leaving the house.

NOTE: The similarity of this formula to the commercial High Gloria Church Incense should be noted, as it is quite likely that this formula is actually an attempt to duplicate this expensive incense formula.

CROWN OF SUCCESS INCENSE   (Corona de Exito)

Benzoin, Lotus, Frankincense, used with a simple ritual prayer will push aside those who hinder your rise to success. It will help stop evil talk and slander, and stop bad vibrations or the envy of your co-workers from affecting you.

Light three white candles in trinity (An equilateral triangle) and burn the incense in the center. Make a sincere prayer for freeing yourself from any negative influence that hinders your success in the world.

CROWN OF SUCCESS POWDER   This powder is used to keep others from being jealous or envious of your position in life, and to promote your advancement, both socially and financially. See Cinnamon Powder, which does about the same thing. Usually an equal limbed cross is made on the forehead, and the remainder of the powder is rubbed on the hands. If a specific person it is desired to block, it may be prayed over by name against them.

>Frankincense – ½ Ounce
>Cinnamon Powder – 1 Ounce
>Orris Root Powder – 1 ½ Ounce

Mix well to obtain a satisfactory blend.

CRUCIBLE OF COURAGE (Crisol de Valor)   A ritual giving people the courage to face difficult situations. The oil is used to anoint purple candles, which are burned with a mention of the particular difficult, frightening, or dangerous situation the person is facing. Millet seed is ground in some sesame oil to make the anointing oil for the candle. The incense is finely ground tobacco powder, like snuff, with a small bit of honey added, burned on charcoal.,

CUBEB SEED   (BERRIES)   [Cubeba officinalis]   [#1734] {Piper Cubeba} Java Berries   A pungent, aromatic, spicy flavored seed, usually picked when unripe. It is used both medicinally and in cooking. Used medically as a mild stimulant and Stomachic.

In magic it is used for its blessing and protective influence, in the same manner as Guinea pepper, with which it is occasionally confused. Used in love potions, incense, sachets and charm bags. Although cubeb smells better that guinea peppers, they are less effective magically as an incense. They may be boiled to impart a pleasant fragrance to the home. The seeds originate in the South Pacific, being exported from Java and the surrounding areas. Often used in commanding or controlling spells, they have some excellent abilities here, but not enough to be as useful as Hi John the Conqueror (Jalap). They are better in love spells than in strictly controlling work.

CUCUMBER   (Echinocystis Lobata)   [# ?]   (Cucurbita Aurantia)   [#793]   The seeds are a natural Psychedelic.   The peeled seedless fruit is rich in Potassium, and is often used in weight loss diets.

CUMMIN   Seed   (Cumino)   (Cuminum Cyminum L.) [#798]   Curry Powder   Burned as incense to insure fidelity, and to break curses.   For peace in the home the seeds should be soaked in water for nine days, and the water used as a sprinkle in the home.   The effect of the incense is doubtful. Ruled by Venus it is used in love potions.   Its best use is to form and hold relationships, thus it is used when a marriage or a family spell is required, rather than just a love or lust spell.   A Veterinary drug.

CUPID   (Cupido)   Another love perfume, this one is made of gum mastic and copal in alcohol, with the scent of your choice added.

CYCLAMEN   [# ?]   Known as the Love plant, it is said to promote a lasting marriage if the living plant is kept in the bedroom.

CYPRESS   See Chypre   The oil is used for financial increase. The wood is used in making magic wands.   Supposedly one of the best money oils there is.

D

DAFFODIL (Narcissus Pseudo Narcissus) [#1558] The bulb is used in black magic as a sedative and a mental paralyzer. It is used in a controlling spell similar to the Santeria spell of Suestro (Theft of the Soul).

DAMASK ROSE INCENSE Same as (Or at least quite similar to) Rose Incense.

DAMBALAH The Male principle of the Universal Life Force in the Voudon religious practice.

DAMIANA LEAVES [Turnera Aphrodisiaca] [#2347] A herb specifically used to improve the sexual function in both men and women. It is quite valuable in clearing away both mental and physical sexual difficulties.

The tea is very cleansing to the aura, and is especially useful in freeing the aura of sexual problems or imbalances. It should be taken by any man past forty as a daily dietary supplement, along with Saw Palmetto to assist in maintaining the health of their sexual organs, as it both balances the female hormones and, assists in preventing male prostate difficulties. The tea is as a slight sexual stimulant, when first taken. Long-term users, especially those who it for more than six months, find that it is strengthening to the reproductive organs in both sexes. (Turnera Diffusa is a natural psychedelic.) Used magically both as an aphrodisiac, as a good luck and love charm, and a laxative.

A domestic good luck charm involves placing some Damania herb in wine, and letting it sit for some time, say three or four hours. The wine is then sprinkled outside the front and back doors of the house, This is said to prevent domestic discord. Another version says that doing this will cause a wandering lover to return, if it is done for twenty-one consecutive days.

DAMNATION POWDER This powder is used magically to lay potent curses. The following ingredients are ground to a fine powder in the mortar:

Three parts of Ferric Ammonium Sulfate, one part of Ocher (Red Iron Oxide), one part of Brimstone (Or flowers of Sulfur) and a half part of Asafetida.

The powder is prayed over and either placed on the person to be cursed, or placed where the person will walk over the powder. It may also be sprinkled on a burning negative incense while the name of the person to be cursed is repeated nine times and the prayer of the curse is being read aloud. The odor of this incense is strong, as is the vibration that it places in the room. I suggest you will probably wish to do this out of doors.

DANDELION Leaves and Root [Taraxicum Dens leonis] [#2265] Used as a blood cleanser and a mild diuretic. It is also used as a stomachic, and in stimulating the liver. Helps eliminate skin diseases.

The root may be carried to make wishes come true. (Sew in a charm bag and wear around the neck.) The tea is supposedly used to induce clairvoyance. The tea is sprinkled on the floor of meeting rooms to make people more harmonious. The juice of the crushed plant is used in head washings, supposedly to make the person become more social. The leaves, especially fresh leaves, are used in salads; and infrequently in food offerings to some of the Orisha and Voudon Loa.

DATURA See Jimson Weed [#845] A narcotic, and poison. The fumes of the burning leaves are used in treating

D

asthma.   A salve made from the leaves is used as a burn ointment.

DEER'S TONGUE   Leaves   Oil   (Liatris Odoratissima) [#1336] Vanilla Leaf   The leaves are used in medicine, the oil in massage, perfumery, and in giving blessings and laying curses. May be used to produce disruptive changes in the astral realms. Works well for changing people's minds. May be used to make people speak freely of things they should not talk of at all.

DELIGHT POWDER   Use to remover inhibitions between lovers.   Praying over Orris Root Powder, and spreading it between the sheets gives the best results, as it opens communication between the lovers.

In the case of casual sexual encounters, a commanding or compelling powder should be used. I do not believe the original "Oriental Delight Powder," a blend with a Vanilla odor is worth making up.

DEMONS   Just as all religion have their saints, and holy men, if only the founder of the denomination, all religions have their demons. This is generally referred to as Goetic magic, and is a field of magic all its own. The worship of these demonic forces is known as demonolatry.

DERECHO   The payment made when entering a graveyard, taking dirt from a grave, or leaving a graveyard. The payment must be made to the, 'Owner of the Cemetery,' who is viewed as the spiritual force that makes it possible for you to leave with no more spirits around you than you came with. This payment is usually a number of pennies, a cigar, or liquor. The payment for this work is dependent on the specifics of the particular religious or magical practice.

DEVIL   (Diablo) An incense that is supposedly used to contact the various demons of Hell. Made from equal quantities of Sulfur and Asafetida that have been mixed together and allowed to stand and blend their influences for a month or so.

Myrrh may be added to bring these demons closer to the person, or even to allow these demons to be summoned to visble appearance. Use the incense liberally, as it usually recuires several tries to conjure up most of the demonic forces.

DEVIL MASTER INCENSE   Used to gain psychic power over those of the opposite sex the person desires. It is a lust incense, not a love or relationship incense. Colchicum root and Vervain make the incense. Use it to fumigate a trace of the person, while making a prayer that you be given domination over them.

DEVIL'S CLAW   (Harpango Procumbens)   [Unknown] Arthritis Root   The secondary root, or tuber, is usually preferred. It is used as a systematic, or general physical, tonic, and may be added to other tonics as a strengthener.

DEVIL'S SHOESTRING   (Colodon Diabalo) [Tephro sia Virginiana] [#2276] The Hoary Pea or Goat's Rue. Used in magic to gain worldly, or material, power over another person, it is used magically for its persistence in effect.

One of the most famous Hoodoo or Voodoo roots, Devils Shoestring is carried for luck in gambling, for protection, for overcoming others, and for many other things. You may prepare small pieces of the root, and carry them in a red charm bag along with other herbs. It is also scattered around the room for the same purpose.

Power over others is usually accomplished through the well-known devils shoestring spell. Camphor, pieces of Devil's Shoestring herb, and Whiskey are placed in a small bottle and mixed well. The mixture is then prayed over. The magician rubs the finished solution on their hands. The person who contacts the magician's hands, usually through a handshake, becomes obedient to the magicians desires.

The oil is made with pieces of the chopped or powdered root in a bottle of mineral oil. It must sit for some time, usually for several months, for the oil to acquire any power from the root.

D

The perfume (Scenta De Diablo) is made from several pieces of the Devils Shoestring root placed in a bottle of alcohol and steeped for a month or more. Alcoholic perfume diluent is better if you really wish to use this as a perfume. The completed perfume has almost no scent, but it will give you a commanding vibration.

DEVIL'S SNUFF POWDER   Used to keep people from interfering in your affairs, and out of your business. It may be placed on your body, or among your private possessions, but it must be prayed over asking for what you want for the best effect. The powder is made of:

One-ounce devil's stinging leaf, ground to a fine powder, one ounce red (Capsicum) pepper. This powder is usually diluted 100:1 with Talcum powder. If you dilute the powder, mix it well and let it set for at least a week or two before using. Only a bit of the powder is ever required.

DEVIL'S SNUFF POWDER   Another version of this powder is used to keep someone from discovering you are working against him or her. The hands are to be dusted with this powder before you cast a spell against an opponent. Any vibration or feeling other than your own may be placed on this powder to place another person's vibration on them. If you can place another vibration on the powder, it will act to identify the other person as the one working against you. If not, it will act as a screen and protect you by obscuring what you are doing.

If you wish you can make up the powder about a half-pound at a time and keep it in the consultation room, so it will adsorb a confusing number of vibrations from your clients.

> Powdered Tobacco - 3 Ounces
> Powdered Orris Root - 3 ounces
> Iron filings - 1 ½ Ounces

Sift together several times and store.

DIGITALIS (Foxglove)   A regulated narcotic, it is used to tone the heart. Famous as one of the plants that modern medicine learned about from rural herbal healers, it is now quite difficult to obtain.

DILL (Eneldo) Seed Leaves (Dill Weed) [Anethum Graveolens] [#192] A nervine, it is used in love potions. The leaves are used as a salad garnish. A tea of the seeds assists in curing hiccups. The seeds are steeped in strong hot wine to make the love potion. It may also be used to counteract negative magic. The seed is used magically to 'put the spirit to sleep' when negative work is to be done on the person.

Supposedly adding a few of the seeds to bath water will make people feel drawn to you. My tendency would be to make up a regular spiritual bath from the seeds

DIRT AS MAGICAL POWDERS   Many varieties of dirt have gained a reputed power of their own, as we may see in the case of the well-known graveyard dirt (which see). There are some other dirt's, or earth's, also used as powders. Below are listed the more popular of these dirt's.

Earth (or dirt) from four street corners, (Or in another case, from seven street corners). Used in Santeria and other African based spiritual practices. If the dirt's are from the corners of four streets in the same city, they may be used to make someone move to that city.

Earth of El Monte, or dirt collected from a mountaintop.

Earth of the Forest, collected from the deep forest, it should be a deep rich black soil. Successfully used in fertility and crop blessing spells.

Earth of the Plaines, collected far from any group of trees, and from a lonely place, this earth is dedicated to "The Lonely Soul," and may be used in prayers dedicated to this dangerous spiritual force. (This is not 'The Lost Soul,' it is a different, but equally dangerous, spiritual force.

Earth (or dust) from four banks, used in money spells.

Earth (or dust) from a prison. Also earth or dirt taken from four jails, used in court spells.

Earth (or dust) from a place of women. This dirt is usually taken from a convent, or the dormitory or classrooms of a woman's school. Considering its usual magical use, it should probably be taken from a brothel.

Earth from an Indian cemetery, is supposedly very powerful stuff indeed.

Also see Goofer Dust, Powders of the Dead, Graveyard Dust.

DITTANY OF CRETE (Origanum Dictamnus) [#1617] Medically it has been used to promote a speedy childbirth, like Pennyroyal. Pregnant women should not take it, as it may cause an abortion.

It is another herb to be mixed with food or drink to kindle love. Formerly used as an incense, where it assists in material manifestation. It is presently hard to find.

DIVINE (Divino) Benzoin will assist a reader in reading for someone. Make it up in an alcoholic form, or with perfume diluant, and anoint the temples before doing a reading.

DIVINATION   In magic the process of the diagnosis of a person's supposed difficulty.

Divination has been well known throughout all human history, as but one example, Reginald Scott in his 1584 'Discoverie of Witchcraft' describes one process of divination with the bible as: "Popish priests ... do practice with a Psalter and keie (key) fastened upon the 49th psalm to discover a theef. And when the names of the suspected persons are orderlie put into the pipe of the keie, at the reading of the words of the psalm ... the book will wagge and fall out of the fingers of him that didst hold it, and he whose name remained in the keie must be the theefe."

This form of divination is known as Bibliomancy, there are several chapters and verses of the bible at which the key may be placed to produce this result.

All spiritual practitioners must be expert in at least one form of divination, as well as being able to read the auric field around a person.

DOGS MERCURY (Mercurialis Perennis) [#1484] Ruled by Mercury, this herb is a deadly poison.

DOGWOOD BARK (Piscidia Erythrina) [#1740] Jamaica Dogwood An acrid sedative and narcotic. Used as a fish poison.

DOGWOOD BARK (Cornus Florida) [#746] Virginia Dogwood The bark and twigs are used as a palo (Palo Emborrachador) It confuses spirits of the dead, and thus makes an excellent sprinkle in either water or alcohol. Used in baths, washes, and as a blow powder. Used in charms to work against another person without their knowledge. As a blow or casting powder, it will confuse spirits, wherever it is placed.

Used in cleansings to remove spirit influences. The twigs are used as palos to confuse people, usually prior to Suestro. A tea made of the flowers makes a fair tonic for female complaints.

DONG QUAI (?) [#?] Primarily used for women's problems, it has a very long history of this use in the orient, where Ginseng is generally used as a food supplement for men, and Dong Quai is used for women.

The herb has a beneficial effect on the female reproductive system, in particular it stimulates and balances the flow of the female hormones. Chinese Ghost workers, when dealing with what they refer to as grandmother ghosts also use a cup of the tea as an offering to the 'Grandmother Ghost' as refreshment, when the Ghost worker is speaking with them.

DOUBLE ACTION (Doble Accion or Doble Efecto) An expediter added to spells to make them work faster. Usually the toxic red Mercuric Oxide, which works best. Toxic yellow mercuric oxide or toxic white mercuric oxide is also used for this purpose. These mercury compounds must be used carefully if at all. A little of them goes a long ways. Do not use them in any incense, as the fumes are toxic, just as the compounds are toxic to the skin. I do not recommend their use under any circumstances.

D

DOVES BLOOD INK   A permanent red ink, best made from crushed pokeberries. This ink is usually used for writing spells of love, affection, and desire.

DRAGONS BLOOD   Gum Resin (Calamus Draco) [#454] (Sangre de Dragon)   An astringent, the solid reed of gum resin is pulverized and used in making bath salts and incense. The powder of the reed is an excellent banishing incense. It may be used to draw all kinds of negative influences from a person. The incense must be used outside, or at least in a room with the windows open. It can transfer negativity from one person to another if it is burned in a closed or confined space. The fumes drive off forces that need to dissipate. For this reason the oil, made from dragon's blood powder and mineral oil, must not ever be used for candle anointing.

Dragon's blood oil may be used as an anointing oil on a person who has been jinxed or crossed.   They should be anointed with a prayer of blessing, preferably after a full spiritual cleansing. The powder is supposed to draw good luck when carried.

The dragon's blood reed is also used as a paint to draw sigils and symbols in ceremonial magic. It is supposed to be used as a charm against impotency, by placing it under the bed. I doubt this use.

DRAW BACK POWDER   This powder is used to reverse the effects of a curse sent to a person, preventing the curse from manifesting. It is to be sprinkled around the house, about a teaspoon of the powder in every room, especially in the corners of rooms.

However, the house must be thoroughly clean, physically and non-physically. In addition, the powder must be changed at the full and new moons. This is done by removing the old powder and replacing it with new.

Gum Camphor – 1 ounce
Frankincense Flour – 1 ounce
Lotus Root Flour – 1 ounce
Orris Root Flour – 1 ounce

Talcum Powder – ¼ ounce
Alum – 1/4 ounce

Mix in the mortar and sift several times. Store in a closed container for a week or so, to allow the materials to blend. Sift again, to gain a good consistency, and put it to use. The powder may be diluted with talc if desired, but it must be sifted wel after each dilution. Thoroughly mixing this powder is very important.

DRAWING POWDER   A powder used unselectively summoning spirits of the human dead. It draws spirits by its virtue alone, so it must be kept in a closed container. It draws spirits so the magician can work with them, and is a very dangerous product for those inexperienced in this work, so the formula is not given.

The occult store product is usually made with iron filings and talcum powder.

DREAM PILLOWS   These are small pillows stuffed with Mullein herb leaves. They are used to promote dreaming in those who wish to learn from their dreams.

DROPWORT   (Oenathe Phellandrium) [#1595]   Water Fennel   This narcotic plant has been used in treating lung ailments.

DULSE   (Rhodymenia Palmata) [#1934]   This seaweed is used in wind and water spells, as well as in love potions.

DUME (Or Doom)   Incense   An incense used for gaining revenge on your enemies. Used in a "Doom" ritual in which three black candles are burned in trinity (An equilateral triangle). The incense, which is burned in the center of the triangle, contains a pinch of graveyard dirt, a teaspoon of millet seed, a teaspoon of sesame seeds, and a pinch of sea salt.

DUME means 'Death Unto My Enemies.'

5

E

EARTH ALCOHOL   (Alcohol Mundo)   Used for gaining favors from the elementals. This is 151 proof alcohol to which has been added either some herb or shavings of a palo. The herb used, or the palo shavings, have been selected signifying the intent desired. They have been prayed over by the person making this alcohol for whatever it is they desire.   Once prepared, the alcohol is given to the earth elementals. This is more of a ritual than a product.

EASY LIFE   (Vida Facil)   This is a perfume made with Jasmine available in an oil, bath or water that is used to calm a person's life. They should take three baths of this kind, over three days, and then wear the perfume for about six weeks. This is appropriate when someone's life becomes too difficult for him or her to deal with. However calming this treatment may be, it is only a temporary solution.

ECHINACEA   (Echinacea Purpurea)   [#?]   Missouri Snake Root   Often called the herbalist's antibiotic; Echinacea is useful in treating all kinds of minor infections.   It increases the functions of the natural immune system, and is good to use for reducing inflammatory and swelling disabilities. Useful in cases of colds, flu, minor infections, and similar difficulties that are not chronic. Often used as a supplement to maintain good health in the cold and flu season, it should be taken daily every other week.

EGYPTIAN BODY   This is an incense made of Natron, Frankincense, and Honey, which is used as a memorial for the dead. Frankincense three parts, Honey two parts, and Natron (Washing Soda) one part. The mixture should digest for at least three months before it is used, to be certain the components are blended together. It has what can best be described as a distinctive odor, so do not use very much of it.

ELECAMPANE   [Inula Helenium]   [# 1221]   Mix the dried powder of the Elecampane root with Vervain and Mistletoe berries to make the ancient true love powder.

Once used medically for lung congestion. This is another love powder that is supposed to be added to the beloved's food or drink. Ruled by Mercury.

ELDER   Berry   Flowers, Leaves, and Roots.   (Samucus Nigra)   [?]   The flowers leaves and roots are used in cases of nasal congestion. Ruled by Venus, it is used to bless or curse as a blow powder. The berries are powdered and used as a protective, placed in the corners of the house. The plant and flowers are discouraging to negative spirit forces in the home.

ELEPHANT   (Alephante) Oil   This is an oil sold to be used to anoint those small plastic elephants that are used as charms. It is just a clear mineral oil as far as I can tell. The oil is also said to be used for other things, I know not what.

ELM BARK   Used to stop slander - Write the name of the one who is slandering you on a piece of elm bark and place it in a small cardboard or wood box. Bury the box somewhere it is unlikely to be disturbed.

ENCHANTMENT   (Encantamieno)   Vervain (Which see) is known as the enchanters herb. It has a long reputation of being the magician's best aid and steady friend. The herb takes a prayer and holds it well. It will go both ways in response to a serious prayer.

76

E

ENCHANTERS NIGHTSHADE (Circaea Lutetiniana) [#640] This herb is used exclusively for occult purposes, as it is considered to be Circe's plant. As such is used in all manner of spells and rituals.

ENDING OIL An oil used to end or terminate things, usually made from Van-Van oil.

The following ending ritual is a common one: Write out the condition to be ended briefly on a piece of paper. Put the paper on a white plate; make three crosses on the plate with red food coloring. Wash the crosses off of the plate with the ending oil, while praying that the condition of situation be ended. make certain that the crosses dissolve into the oil. Save the oil, which now has the red food coloring in it. Put the plate and the paper into the garbage. You may now use the oil to bring an end to the condition in any way you wish.

ENVY AND JEALOUSY POWDER This powder is used to put an end to feelings of envy and jealousy between people. A casting powder, it is placed where the jealous person to be affected will walk.

Sweet Basil – 1 ounce
Rosemary – 1 ounce

EPHEDRA (Ephedra Sinica) (or equisentina) The stems are used for the relief of asthma and hay fever. The domestic herb is Ephedra Nevadensis.

ERYNGIUM (Eryngium Maritimum) Sea Holly [#929] The root is used. Aids in suppressed menstruation and in urinary disorders. Used in some love potions, it is ruled by the Moon.

EUCALYPTUS Leaves (Eucalyptus Globulus) [#944] Used for treating sore throats, bacterial infections of the lungs, and as a flea and fly repellent. As a healing herb, it keeps astral negativity under control. An antiseptic herb, the tea is a cleansing sprinkle as well as a useful; bath or wash for the ill or bedridden.

It is said to be protective, but I have no experience of its protective qualities. The bath is calming and healing, as well as mildly cleansing. The leaves are often put into the pillows of those who wish to avoid illness.

EUPHORBIA   (Euphorbia Hirta) [# ?] {Euphorbia Pilulifera}   Also known as asthma weed, it is a remedy for coughs, bronchial or pulmonary disorders, and paroxysmal asthma. (Euphorbia Ipecacuanha) [#973]   The bark of the root is an emetic, known as Wild Ipecac. Used in treating Dropsy and as a casting powder, but it does not take a magical charge very well at all.

EVE OIL   A powerful aphrodisiac, made of the woman's own sexual fluids which are added to the perfume of her choice. The perfume is then ritually worked by the spiritual practitioner or magician, and returned to the woman. The woman must use it sparingly and with great care. Usually used to increase the sexual interest of a woman's husband.

EVENING PRIMROSE   (OEnothera Biennis) [#1596] The bark and leaves are used in relieving asthma and whooping cough.   An astringent and sedative.   The oil is good for postmenopausal women to stabilize their hormonal level. Often taken as an oil capsule, or as the herbal powder.

EVIL EYE   (Mal Ojo or Mal de Ojo - Malochia)   Perfume oil made in the name of the person who is to use it to protect themselves from the evil eye. Usually bluish in color, made of mineral oil. The person places a bit of the oil on their hands each day for seven days to grant them protection from the evil eye. The protection, once gained, will last from six months to a year.

EYEBRIGHT   [Euphrasia Officinalis]   [#980]   Ruled by the Sun in Leo. In Christian lore, it is the herb of the archangel Michael. The leaves are used as an eyewash, it is made into a tea and used twice daily to wash the eyes to strengthen them. It s also recommended for both sinus and catarrh. The medical

E

dosage is a teaspoon of the herb to a half pint of boiling water. Brew covered for fifteen minutes then strain and drink.

Slightly astringent, it promotes cleansing. The herb tea specifically strengthens the cornea, or outer part of the eye, and thus assists in developing better vision. Eyebright is also used in developing the astral sight, by following the same practice of twice daily eye washings. Burned as an incense in the bedroom before sleeping it is said to increase the depth and truth of the sleepers dreams.

EXORCISM (Exorcismo) Oil, Incense, and Powder Many of the products for exorcism are made up for the occasion. Usually these products have a high vibration, and make haunting or possessing forces and negative spirits uncomfortable. For general exorcism work, Frankincense and Benzoin are good choices as incenses. Avoid using Myrrh, or any incenses containing Myrrh for exorcisms, as it strengthens any astral force involved. The best powders and oils for exorcism are those listed under blessing or anointing.

EXPEDITERS' Elemental mercury, and the oxides of mercury are used extensively in magic as expediters. Red mercuric oxide is actually the best of the mercuric expediters, however all of the mercuric oxides are as toxic as mercury itself. There are several vegetable expediters, celery seed being the most effective one. So-called fern seed, the spores of the king or giant fern, and lycopodium powder are also excellent expediters.

Because mercury and its oxides are a slow cumulative poison, they should not be used. Cinnabar, the ore from which mercury is extracted, is also toxic. There is no way around it, the safe magician will not use either mercury or its ores as expediters in practicing magic. They are too dangerous over time.

F

FANTASY   (Fantasia)   Another love oil.   Most of the orcinary botanica and occult store oils fit this description, as they contain little in them that can do what they say they will do.

FAST LUCK   (Suerte Rapido)   Oil, Perfume, Powder Cinnamon powder, Vanilla bean powder, and powdered wintergreen, the oil is best a plant oil, Almond oil probably being the best choice. The oil may be diluted in a perfume oil medium, or the aged powder may be added to a favorite perfume.   Not a compelling oil, this increases the attraction people feel toward the person wearing it. The powder is to be applied to the sternum.

FAST LUCK   (Suerte Rapido)   Oil, Incense, Powder, Sprinkle, and Floor Wash   Used when fast luck, or a sudden change of the atmosphere is needed.   This may be any lightening compound, or mixture, such as the above, which may be applied to rid an area of negative vibrations.

However, when faced with this problem, a heavy thought form eliminator incense should be used as soon as possible, to rid the area of the heavier thoughts.   Then the entire place should be physically cleaned and worked on spiritually.   Mint

F

and rum compounds are often used as fast luck compounds, especially in floor washes. If you really want to change the vibration of the place, the more thorough work is much better, as it has longer lasting results.   Once you have it cleaned out, to put a new vibration in, use the powder or oil above with a floor wash made of Alkanet root tea added to the wash water.

FAST SCRUBBING INCENSE MIXTURE   Used to astrally scrub negative vibrations from a place, quickly and efficiently. May be made from a blend of brown sugar, dried egg yoke powder, and a pinch of table salt.   Burn the mixture on charcoal, and carry it throughout the place to be scrubbed astrally. It works much better than it smells.

FAST SUCCESS (Exito Rapido)   Water, Oil, Perfume, A blend or mixture of honeysuckle perfume and cinquefoil with mint herbs in water, oil, or perfume diluent. In the case of the water or perfume, the herbs are left in the bottle, while the perfume often has a honeysuckle flower in it.

FENNEL SEED   [Anethum Foeniculum (Officinale)] [#1003] {Foeniculum Vulgare}   Young fennel shoots are often used as a vegetable. One of the nine sacred herbs of the early Saxons, it was believed to have the power to combat the nine causes of disease.   Used as an aid to digestion, and often provided after meals in the Middle East and India for this purpose.

The tea is a good eyewash, it also relieves the stomach of gas and acidity.   Used to increase the menstrual flow.   In Europe a sprig of the plant is carried to protect the person from witchcraft. It is also used in love potions, and as an aphrodisiac in wine or strong tea. Venus Rules this useful herb.

FENUGREEK SEED   (Alholua)   [Trigonella Foenum Graecum L.]   [#2336] One of mankind's oldest cultivated plants, it is used as a spice as well as a food stuff. One of the constitutes of the Egyptian KUPHI or holy smoke used in fumigation's, and in embalming as an incense.   The seed powder is used as a yellow dyestuff.   The seeds are eaten either raw or boiled, often with honey. The powdered seeds themselves are used to restore the mentation of an individual who is over stressed, or who suffers from 'brain fag,' nervous exhaustion.

Used as a head wash, to strengthen the mentation process, the tea is also used as a stomachic, for settling the stomach and bringing the digestive process back to normal. The tea has a good effect on the throat and bowels. Makes a good poultice for wounds or bites. Helps to clear mucous congestion. It is a component of almost all of the Voudon and other head washes used in various magico-religious initiations, where it is a specific for clearing the mentation process. Mercury Rules it, as might be expected.

FERN   Ferns planted at the front door and windows of a house are supposed to protect the house from witchcraft. My grandmother was a firm believer in this practice, tending her ferns as well as her flowers.

FEVERFEW   (Pyrethrum   Parthenium)   [#1864] {Tanacetum Parthenium} A good general tonic. Relieves cold and flue symptoms. It is said to protect from sickness and accident when carried on the person.

FIERY COMMAND   (Ardiente Orden) Incense   This is actually a spell used to reinforce a commanding oil or other formulation that has been prepared for a person.

Three candles are burned in trinity, (In an equilateral triangle shape) around the oil, or other formulation, which has been placed in the center of the triangle. The material is commanded to serve the person who is to use it. Any incense suitable to the nature of the purpose of the product may be burned during this ritual. This is a way of powerfully extending the charge of the commanding oil or other product being prepared for someone.

FIERY WALL OF PROTECTION   (Ardiente Padre de Protection) This is a spell used to protect a person. This spell uses a small amount of gunpowder, and is usually worked by a spiritual practitioner on a person following a spiritual cleansing by the practitioner.   The incense used is usually sage and tobacco, the person is censed with it.

FIERY WALL OF PROTECTION POWDER   This powder is used to prevent anyone from placing a curse on the person using it.   It may be sprinkled around the walls of a house, or even included in the masonry or paint coating of the wall.   It has a very protective influence wherever it is placed.

Take one ounce of compelling powder and add:

> Rosemary powder - ¼ ounce
> Cinnamon - ¼ ounce
> Cloves - ½ ounce

Sift well several times, and pray over the powder for what is desired.

FIRE OF LOVE POWDER   Used for spells of love and passion, it creates a strong desire.   A commanding or compelling powder is best for seduction, as this powder only creates desire.   Only a bit of the powder is required, placed discretely on the person in whom desire is raised.

> Patchouli Powder - ½ Ounce
> Orris Root Powder - ½ Ounce
> High Conquering Powder - ¼ Ounce

Sift together several times to get an even blend.   Keep covered in a dark place when not in use.

FIVE CIRCLE (Cinco Circulos)   Incense, Oil   Said to be a psychic developer, it is to be used in the bedroom, and applied to the forehead before sleep.   It is only to be used in small amounts.   Made from Benzoin in a perfume oil diluent.   The incense is straight benzoin, burned on charcoal.

FIVE FINGER GRASS   (Mano Pondoroso) [Poten-tilla Canadensis] [#1808]   See Cinquefoil   The tea is often used as a hand and head wash before performing Voodoo or Hoodoo rituals.   As a head wash it should be used in conjunction with other herbs, usually including fenugreek.   The head wash cleans away negative influences, as does the mouthwash and gargle made from this herb. Five-finger grass is placed in a red handkerchief and put at the head of the bed, under the mattress or tied on the bed frame, to ward off evil in the night.

Used in charm bags to assist people in getting their way. Opens communications, making the person who carries it speak more eloquently. It is not a commanding or compelling ingredient. The bath cleans negativity away from the person. To make someone speak his or her mind, place the herb on a piece of paper on which you have written the person's name and pray over it for the effect you desire.

FISH BERRIES   A toxic seed that is used to restore sexual potency in men. It is not very efficient in my opinion.

FIT ROOT   (Monototropa Uniflora)   [#1519]   Ice Plant   Anti spasmodic, nervine. Aids in the reduction of fevers.

FLAX SEED   (Linum Usitatissimum)   [#1364]   Used as a tea to increase the powers of divination. This supposed remedy is of dubious value. The seed has also been used mechanically, to clear the eyes of dirt or mucous. May be used to cause fights between married couples if added to other cursing ingredients in a tea, and sprinkled on their doorstep.

FLEABANE   (Erigeron Canadense)   [#919]   An astringent tonic and diuretic, it is used for the removal of curses, as well as fleas.

FLORIDA WATER   [Agua Florida]   A commercial product made by Lanman & Kemp Barclay & Co. of Westwood, NJ. This is the best known of the various Florida Waters. The water, actually a cologne, is spiritually cleansing, as it is repulsive to negative spiritual entities. It contains the essence of Kananga flowers, also known as Ylang Ylang, (which see) an oil originally used to hide the odor of paint drying.

F

FLOR de MUERTO   (Flower of the dead)   Marigold, which see. It receives this name because a tea of marigold can bae used to strengthen the spirit of the human dead.

FLY   (Mosca) Oil, Powder   Used to make a person feel very uncomfortable indeed. It is made from a collection of dried flies, and often other insects, which are ground up and prayed over for the purpose. The oil used is mineral oil. It should be applied to a trace of the person, which is then prayed over for the effect desired.

FLOOR WASHES   The following floor washes may be used as indicated: For a residence: Rain water, Creosote oil, White sugar, Cinnamon powder, Parsley, (soak a bunch of Parsley in rain water, in the refrigerator, for three or four days. Strain it out before using. Mix up about a gallon of the solution and mop the floors of the house with it.

For a place of Business: Rain Water, Creosote Oil, Mucha Gente Oil (Many People Oil), White sugar, Parsley, as above, Cinnamon, Jasmine oil, Ammonia, and Camphor.   Used as above.

FLYING DEVIL POWDER   A strong uncrossing powder, used to break or remove a curse or hex. It can be used in almost any situation. Used as a blow powder for these conditions, it may also be used as a casting powder, or placed in the corners of a room. This powder must be used with care. It is a complicated powder, but one that is very effective when it is made and used properly.

Two different elements must be made up.

> Powdered white eggshells - 2 ounces
> Powdered Arrowroot - 2 ounces
> Powdered Lotus Root - 2 ounces

Sift together several times and store in a closed bottle.

The second material to be made up is:

> Magnesium Carbonate - ½ ounce
> Calcium Carbonate - ¼ ounce
> Ground Nutmeg - ¼ level teaspoon

Powdered Cinnamon - ¼ teaspoon
Ground Cloves - ½ teaspoon
Fine Iron filings - ¼ teaspoon

Sift together several times so they are well mixed. Then Add to this mixture:

Powdered soapstone – 1 heaping Tablespoon, (4 teaspoons full)

Mix thoroughly and sift several times to distribute the soapstone throughout the mixture. Store the second mixture in an amber bottle and store away for a week or so after adding a drop of holy water.

When you are ready to prepare the mixture, either on the new Moon or within two days afterwards, pour the first mixture into a white bowl, and pray over it, asking that it become the agent for the removal of evil and negativity. Bless the mixture three times and stir in the contents of the second mixture, praying that it defend the person place or thing it is used on from anything that is evil, malicious, harmful, hateful, or negative. Bless the final mixture three times, and store it away in a light tight container. It must be kept out of the light, and best out of sight.

To use it to remove curses, blow it from your hand onto the person who is to be unhexed.

FOOLS PARSLEY (Aethusa Cynapium) [#77] Dog Poison In small quantities it is a stomach sedative. However, it must be used with great caution, as it is poison and narcotic.

FOOT PRINT MAGIC More common among the African American Hoodoo community than among those who derived their magic from European sources, Footprint magic uses the footprint of someone as their magical 'trace.' In some cases, the footprint itself may be 'worked' as in the following spell from the Lancaster, PA area.

To Keep A Trespasser Off Of Your Land

Nail the trespasser's footprint with a large nail when you see them walking on your land. Say the following as you push the nail into the earth. "May your body come here no more, but your spirit remain to guard the crop that grows on this land until your body has been seven years dead!"

F

FO TI TIENG (Hydrocoytle Asiaticus Minor) Herb taken as a general tonic, it has rejuvenation qualities, clearing the astral body. It is considered by some to be an aphrodisiac, but its primary function is clearing the astral body.

I have been told this is another herb with the new name applied. It is generally known as FO-TI, which is less expensive than Fo-Ti Tieng. In any event, my source for this herb has dried up, and I can no longer obtain it, so it really does not matter what it is.

FOR A MAN TO LOVE YOU This perfume and incense are used with a ritual to tie a man to a woman. It is a flowery orange blossom scent. The incense has orange zest and Myrrh in it.

FORTUNE TELLER (Madama or Adivino) Used by those who read fortunes for others to assist them in seeing things more clearly. Tiger Balm ointment rubbed sparingly on the temples and the third eye point on the forehead will assist in this effect.

FOUR HOT SPICES VINEGAR A Vinegar used to heat up a situation, or to add heat to someone's life. Made of apple cider vinegar, garlic, mustard, red pepper, and ground black pepper. It may be used to heat up the life of someone whose life is a bit slow moving by writing their name on a piece of paper with a pencil. Place the paper into a small bottle, add the vinegar to it, pray over this for what you want for the person, and close the bottle. Now bury the bottle in the ground somewhere. It can go both ways, so what you want for the person may be either good or bad.

FOUR THIEVES VINEGAR - FOUR THIEVES WINE (Vinagree de Quatro Rateros, or Cuarto Ladrones) This is actually an all heal, made from red wine, or red wine vinegar, and garlic. It has an interesting history, mentioned below. Magically, it is used in a number of ways, the most predominate one is getting people out of your life. For this use, the name of the person you wish to rid yourself of is written on a piece of paper, and placed in a small bottle of the vinegar. The bottle is then thrown into a river with a prayer they leave your life.

The formula dates from the fifteenth century, possibly even before then, when it first came to light as a healing formula. When the bubonic plague raged through Europe in the 1400's, the number of people dying in a town in southern France so overwhelmed the gravediggers they called upon the municipal authorities for assistance. Four thieves, who had been jailed together were released on the condition they assist in burying the dead. They served so well at their gruesome task that when the plague passed, they were pardoned on the condition they left town and never returned.

As they were being pardoned, one of the magistrates asked them how they had managed to appear to remain so healthy, even though they had been burying those who died of the plague. The thieves told the magistrate that they took bottles of cheep red wine, filled them with peeled garlic, and allowed them to stand for a few days, which caused the wine to begin to turn to vinegar. The thieves then drank a wineglass full with every meal. They continued to do this for the three or four months they had been engaged in burying the dead, and for some time afterwards.

Four Thieves Wine Is Made The Following Way

A bottle of Burgundy (red) wine is divided between two bottles, and both bottles are filled with peeled and occasionally crushed, garlic cloves. The bottles are placed in the refrigerator or the springhouse for a week or so. Two ounces of the wine, possibly on the way to becoming vinegar, are taken twice or three times each day.

During the 1917 flue epidemic my grandfather used this mixture on all of his family, including the infants. None of the family became ill, although there were several deaths in the rural neighborhood where he lived.

A wineglass (2 fluid ounces or so) in the bathtub is a good precaution against malochia. It will only last until the next bath, which is no excuse for not bathing.

F

FOUR WINDS (Cuatro Vientos) Incense   Used to dissipate something, as if you were blowing it to the four winds. This incense contains equal amounts of gum mastic, copal, and frankincense. The expediter for this incense is red pepper.

FOXGLOVE (Digitalis Purpurea) [#863] The leaves are used as a cardiac tonic. It must be used with caution as it has a cumulative effect, and an overdose can be fatal. A regulated narcotic, and poison, it was one of the ingredients of the witches flying ointments.

FRANKINCENSE (Boswellia Serrata) [#405] (Incienso Olibano)   Indian Olibanum, or male incense, it relates to the Sun. It is a natural gum resin product, extracted from the tree. One of mankind's oldest incenses, it has been burned as an offering to the gods for thousands of years. Another incense used extensively since ancient times in both religion and magic.

FRENCH LOVE POWDER   A body powder of Talc with vanilla powder or perfume in it. The powder has a very good reputation among professional women, who have used it successfully for well over a hundred years.

FRENCH OIL (Frances)   This is actually an oil used in trade, but I have no idea what it is except that it is a clear oil of low viscosity.

FRIENDSHIP (Amistad) Incense, Oil Try burning a little bit of cinnamon and coriander in your home before friends arrive. An oil of these herbs also works well in making friends and acquaintances.

G

GALANGAL   [Alpina Galanga] [#116] Chewing High John (De Galingale) The root is used.   The powder of the root is to be burned every night for fourteen nights before going to court. Save the ashes in a chamois skin bag, and take the bag to court with you. It makes for a more favorable verdict from judge or jury.

Used as incense in ritual and ceremonial magic, the root is also a well-known Middle Eastern and Oriental seasoning. The root is sometimes carried as a good luck charm.

GALBANUM   (Ferula Galbaniflua) [#997] Gum Resin A stimulant and resolver used in the treatment of hysteria. Gum Galbanum is used in incenses as well, where it affects the mentation. See also Goats Rue, (Buron Galbanifera) [#422] Galega Officinalis.

GATHERING HERBS   One of the reasons for finding the planet ruling an herb is to effectively time when it is to be gathered. According to the 17th century astrologer Richard Ball, ... "It is also necessary that the Planet governing the herb you gather be the ruler of the day, as well as the ruler of the hour. For example: Suppose you gather herbs governed by the Moon, Monday being assigned her government, that day is most

G

proper to gather her herbs in, having regard to the Hour she rules the same day, which is every Monday at Sunrise. The like you may observe of all the herbs gathered by the planets," ... ...

Richard Ball, Astro-Physical Compendium, London 1697 (Ballantrae undated reprint - Page 112.

Another excellent traditional resource in this regard is Culpepper's herbal.

GARDENIA   Oil, Perfume, Floor Wash, Water, Spray, Sprinkle   Used to improve a marriage or other sexual relationship. It has a very good reputation in this area. All of the above products are made from the (usually artificial) essential oil.

GARLIC   (Ajo) [Allium Sativum L.] [#105] Ruled by Mars in Aries.   Garlic is the primary anti infection remedy and heart medicine of the European and Mediterranean herbalist. It is a direct blood purifier, working to reduce high blood pressure, as well as to remove impurities from the blood stream by strengthening the liver. The bad reaction that many people have to garlic is an indication of their need to purify their blood stream. Crushed and rubbed on the soles of the feet, it will reduce the highest fevers.

To keep money in the house, burn the skin covering garlic cloves in the kitchen fire, or on charcoal if you don't have an open fire in your kitchen.

As a bath, or head wash, garlic will remove stuck conditions, minor crossings, and mental blockages, from people. As a tea it assists the patient in recovering from any illness, but it is especially good for internal disorders, such as ulcers of the stomach, throat problems, and intestinal inflammations of any kind. It will also assist in conquering colds or flu. It also increases the perspiration and urination. Three cloves of garlic a day is the usual dose recommended. This dose will guarantee you privacy if nothing else.

Garlic is the primary ingredient in four thieves' wine or vinegar. (Which see)   It has too many uses in magic to mention. In general it is used to ward off evil and keep malefic forces away.

Garlic is also an ingredient in a number of incense formulas. Aligned with Mars in Aries, it removes heavy thought forms wherever it is burned. A blend of Garlic and Onion powders is often burned to clear areas of heavy negativity. Equal parts of Garlic, Dark Brown Sugar, and Coffee will remove the heaviest and most depressing astral thought forms from the place it is burned. For the purification of a house, an incense of peeled garlic cloves, Myrrh, Benzoin, Bay Leaves, and Brown sugar is burned. Garlic is so often used in folk magic and healing that there have been several books written exclusively about its use.

GENTIAN ROOT (Gentiana Lutea) [#1050] Also called Baldmony. A calmative, and aid to digestion. It brings on menstruation, and should not be used by pregnant women. Ruled by Mars.

GERMICIDES The oils of Cinnamon, Clove, Garlic, Oregano, and Sage, all have germicidal properties. Honey is the perfect germicide, and should replace sugar in your tea and coffee to improve your health.

GET AWAY POWDER To be sprinkled in the path of anyone you wish to stop bothering you. The powder will turn people away on contact. Place a pinch of the powder on window ledges, and on the front doorstep to discourage people as well.

The powder is made from two parts flowers of Sulfur, one part Red Cayenne pepper powder, a pinch of Asafetida, and five parts of powdered Arrowroot. Pray over this powder, after mixing, and then let it sit for several days. Make the prayer again, as you apply the powder to where you wish to place it to discourage others.

GET AWAY POWDER ESCAPE POWDER Used to help a person escape from bad situations. It turns pursuers away from the person using the powder. It must be prayed over by name for the desired purpose.

G

To end a neighbor's curiosity about your affairs, you can mix some of this powder with a pinch of iron filings, and pray over it. Put a bit of this powder on the windowsills of each of your windows that face outside your property. Renew this about every six months. This is a very useful powder for those who do this work.

> Licorice root powder - 1 ounce
> Arrowroot powder - ½ ounce
> Orrisroot powder - ½ ounce
> Talcum Powder - ½ ounce

Mix thoroughly by sifting several times. Use as a casting powder, casting behind the person whose path is to be obscured.

For this purpose also see, Poplar powder, and Devil's shoestring powder.

GHOST MONEY [Hell money]   In oriental practice, especially among the Chinese, the departed are given 'Hell Money,' which is often physically spread around their grave site. Alternatively, it may be burned to them for their use in the other world. Sometimes, the offering of food and drink to the departed, along with offerings of 'Hell Money,' are made. The most active of these spirits of the departed are said to be 'hungry ghosts.' In hungering for their earthly experiences they find their greatest suffering.

GINGER ROOT (Jengibre) [Zingiber Officinale Rose.] [#2463] Ruled by Mars. Ginger root is a primary body heater, stimulating the triple heater meridian of the acupuncturist. It may be taken either as candied ginger, ginger tea, or in the form of a ginger pack, or a poultice. As a tea, it excites the digestive action and loosens mucus in the throat and the bronchial tract.

Ginger may be used to apply heat to any part of the body, as it quickly penetrates the entire physical system. Ingested as a food it quickly restores balance to a person who requires warmth, or a better energy flow. The tea and ginger jellies or candied ginger should be given to someone with low body temperature (Hypothermia) as soon as they can eat. It relieves upsets, gas, and general stomach discomfort.

Its most popular use is as an anti nausea medication for motion sickness. One gram of ginger powder will relieve nausea in 80% of the human population with no side effects at all. It is also useful to thin the blood, something that requires about five grams of the powder, per dose, in five doses, each day. This treatment is continued each day for several weeks until the proper clotting level (by test) is reached. It will also assist in opening up blood flow to the minor capillaries of the body.

GINGER JELLIES

2 Oz Gelatin, 4 1/3 Cup of granulated Sugar, 8 Oz Fresh Ginger, peeled, and coarsely chopped. Powdered sugar for rolling the finished ginger candies in.

Soften gelatin in two cups of water. Add sugar and allow to warm, stirring with spoon until sugar dissolves. Increase heat and bring to a boil. Add ginger. Reduce heat and boil steadily for fifteen minutes. Let stand for ten minutes, then pour through a strainer into a prepared oiled 8-inch square pan. Let sit for 24 hours. Cut ginger jelly into cubes, and roll in powdered confectioners sugar. Will keep in a plastic container for about two months.

Magically, ginger is a catalyst, when added to incense it will enhance the effect of the incense, making it work more quickly. While it is almost always the smallest part of any spell by volume, it is an expediter and a catalyst that will assist in promoting the action of any incense, or herbal spell. It may be used in baths as well, along with other herbal ingredients.

Ginger, Crystallized - Sugar coated Ginger slices. Used primarily as a foodstuff. Ginger may be added to ritual bonfires to summon spirits to watch the ritual.

GINKO BILOBA   [Salisburia Adiantifolia] [#2008] A more recently popular herb, Ginko Biloba is used in Europe to treat, and gain remission from, Alzheimer's disease and senile dementia. It improves the body's peripheral blood circulation,

G

especially the circulation of blood to the brain and small capillaries.

It aids by supplying nutrients to collagen in the joints, thus is effective in treating some arthritis and rheumatism problems. Because it improves the circulation of blood to the brain, it also assists in relieving anxiety and tension. Short-term memory loss is frequently halted after a months use, as are the mood swings associated with senile dementia. This is another herb that must be continued on long-term usage to have the best effect. The best results are usually found after a year's continual usage. Daily dose is 40 mg to 100 mg tablets of the extract, taken three times a day.

The oil of the Ginko fruit is used in therapeutic massage lotions.

GINSENG   [Panax Quinquefolia]   [#1649]   {Panax Ginseng}   One of the most famous trade herbs of both ancient and modern times, Ginseng is taken to increase the body's natural energy.

It is a multi purpose herb, a gentle stimulant that remains beneficial over many years of use. The Chinese call it the root of long life. It assists in supporting the bodies natural immune system, and has generally tonic benefits on the whole human constitution. It is useful in digestive disturbances, and for the promotion of the appetite. If taken when hot, as in a tea, it will promote perspiration. Used for lung and stomach troubles as well. It has a reputation as a male aphrodisiac, but is good for both men and women. Three to nine grams a day is the usual dose. The tonic is made from the root, macerate the root and steep in brandy for at least three weeks. Drink a wine glass full every night.

GLEDITSCHTA   (Gleditschia Triacanthos) [#1073] Honey Locust   The sap contains sugar, cocaine, and atropine. Heavy use of this sap produces a stupor and the loss of reflex action. St. John the Baptist was said to have lived on this herb.

GOATS MILK   Particularly suited to those who are bed-ridden, or who have poor digestion. It is used to wash the sexual organs to add vigor to them. The milk is used in treating arthritis and inflexibility of the arms and joints of the body by applying it as a compress. It has a slightly higher fat content than cow's milk.

GOAT'S RUE HERB   (Tephrosia Virginiana)   [#2276] Devils Shoestring, which see.   Also see Galega Officinalis [#422] Buron Galbanifera - the source of Gum Galbanum.

GOD FIRE   An expediter made of crushed celery seed and any other relevant herbs, added to spells to hasten their operation. In rituals, it is best burned on charcoal.

GODDESS   (Diosa)   Each of the many goddesses has their own incenses, attributes, offerings, and so forth.   You must know these before you start making offerings or promises to any of them. It is possible to get into a lot of trouble by making the wrong offerings to a deity.

GOLD AND SILVER   (Oro Y Plata)   Oil   Made with real gold and silver foil, along with other ingredients, this oil is used as a money drawing oil. I do not have a complete formula for this oil.

GOLDEN SEAL   Root   [Hydrastis Canadensis]   [#1177] Used in mouthwashes, and in many other ways, the root has an undeserved reputation for general healing. It is another tonic herb, of which there are a great many. It is a bacteriastatic herb, but not to any great extent. Ruled by the Sun, the root has the influence of Saturn.   Best given in tea, it's most effective use is in making an eye ointment. It is sometimes used as a constituent of prosperity incense. Used with Myrrh to strengthen the mucus membranes and heal ulcerated sores. Golden Seal tea is an excellent floor wash for business places.

GOLDTHREAD   (Coptis Trifolia)   [#729]   Used as a mouthwash, and a tea for ulcers. The tea is good for healing canker sores.

G

GOOD LUCK MYSTIC POWDER   This powder allows a person to have true dreams, which are to assist them to solve problems in their life.

> Cinnamon powder – 1 ounce
> Vanilla extract 2 or 3 drops
> Yerba Santa herb ¼ teaspoon
> Jonquil Bulb Powder ¼ teaspoon

Sift together several times to mix well. Set aside for two weeks to allow the ingredients to blend, and sift to mix again. To use, sprinkle about your room, and between the sheets of your bed.

GOOD LUCK SPIRITUAL POWDER   An herbal powder used in some Spanish Afro Catholic Magical Religious practices to bring good luck into the life. It is used as a blessing and uncrossing powder. It is occasionally sprinkled on altars and rubbed on the hands of those attending rituals.

The powder is made from any of the several plants known as Yerba Santa and Yerba Buena.

GOOFER DUST   A frequently used Hoodoo or Root Working powder. The powder is used in many ways, primarily for cursing others. In some formulations it is only graveyard dirt, (Which see) in other formulations it is composed of graveyard dirt and a number of ingredients, often including sulfur and powdered snakeskin, and occasionally other parts of the snake. As these formulations are all local, there seems to be no one agreed on composition for this material.

Powdered spiders and other powdered dead insects are also added to make a 'goofer dust' formula, as are, red pepper, snail shells, and other ingredients. The powder is used to make people leave the user alone, or to make them leave a particular place, such as to make them leave home.

GOONA GOONA (Golona Golona) Incense   Used to create an atmosphere of trust and understanding in an area, thus bringing people closer together.

Made of the clear copal incense known as Palm or Pom incense. When the incense is burning, light a purple candle and make a prayer for the solution of any difficulty. It is often used for peaceful home prayers, and for solving marital problems. For meetings, it should be burned before or while the meeting is in progress.

GOTU KOLA HERB [Unknown] [?] A specific for increasing the clarity of the mental body and revitalizing the nervous system. Gotu Kola must not be taken within four hours of taking Vitamin C. It increases the circulation of blood to the brain, and is an excellent general tonic for the nervous system. It may increase the ability to learn in some people, especially those who have a blocked mentation. Long-term use is required for the best results.

GRAINS OF PARADISE [Amomum Granum Paradisi] [#138] Guinea Peppers, a trade item in West Africa, from where the idea that they were a powerful magical spice came from. Also known as Paradise Seed.

Used in West African, and some South American, cooking they are usually a substitute for Black Pepper.

As a love stimulant, the grains are added to food and drink. They are also often carried in a red charm bag for luck, with or without other herbs. In some cases they are used to add power to the charm bags. Seven of the Grains of Paradise are steeped in boiling water and used to make a bath for men who are having trouble gaining the affectations of women.

The grains are used in the spell of the two saints, in which a picture of St. Peter is put at the front door, and a picture of St. Michael is put at the back door. Charm bags, containing grains of paradise are placed behind each of the two pictures, to guarantee success in the home. This is called feeding the saints. The charm bags of grains of paradise are replaced about every three months or so.

The peppers may be prayed over and cast upon the steps of a house to break up a home. They are often burned, to protect against conjure and hexes. They are fed to the saints for success, as explained above.

98

G

To cause harm to an enemy: Scorch a rabbit's foot in fire, and place it on a new piece of black cloth. Sprinkle it with Guinea Pepper and graveyard dirt. Place on top of this, face down, a photograph of the enemy, or a piece of parchment on which you have written the enemy's name, backward, in black ink. Fold up the parcel, and tie it with a piece of black twine or yarn. Now bore a hole on the west side of a tree on your enemies property, or as close to his home as is possible. Hide your charm in this hole. As the sun goes down each day, your enemy will become weaker and weaker.

TO CAUSE DEATH BY ENCHANTMENT

Place into a jar some vinegar, some Guinea Peppers, a wolf's heart, and the victim's name, which you have written on parchment paper with dragon's blood ink. At Midnight on a Friday night, light a black candle for illumination and shake the jar thirteen times, while cursing your foe:

_____ (Name of Enemy) _____,
I curse thee unceasingly,
May your bones break painfully,
May your mind wander aimlessly,
May your skin rot in agony,
May your heart die of jealousy,

Bury the jar upside down in the nearest graveyard. Within thirteen days, your enemy will either perish or vanish from your sight.

GUINEA   (Guienea)   A series of powder and oil products are made from the Guinea peppers described above. They are used for a variety of things, mostly for stimulating or starting things.

GRAPE   (Vitis Vinifera)   [#2440]   Grapes are the fruit of the vine, or the fruit of the tree of life. They are symbols of the universal life force.

While the tea of grape vine bark is somewhat protective in baths, the vine itself is used in laying hexes and curses on others. Sun dried grapes are raisins, and are symbols of the

Sun. Raisins are used in some ancient religious incense mixtures. (Usually along with honey, and sometimes Frankincense.)

The corkscrew like pieces of the grape vine may be used in love spells. They are dried, powdered, and put into food that the beloved is to eat. They have other uses in magic as well. Charcoal of the grape vine is also used in magic, especially in making magic powders. See Charcoal, for their use in healing.

Grape leaf tea is used as a sprinkle to protect a home from hexes. Grape wine is used for this purpose in some temples.

GRAVEYARD DUST or DIRT (Polvo de Muerto, Polvo de Cemetario) Graveyard dirt, Graveyard Mystic Powder, all of these are correctly made from dirt taken from a grave, preferably the grave of a lover, or a parent. The dirt is supposed to have some connection to the spirit of the person buried in the grave, but often does not have any connection to any spirit connected with the person using the graveyard dirt at all.

True graveyard dirt, or cemetery dirt, is just dirt taken from a cemetery. Unless you have taken the dirt yourself you have no real assurance of its provenance. Even then, the power of the dirt is of dubious value, unless you have tied a spirit to it for some purpose. This is not as easy a task as it sounds.

This work usually involves giving the spirit whom you wish to tie to the earth an offering, usually of liquor, such as whiskey or rum. In some practices the location on the grave from which the dirt is taken is important as well. Some authorities say it must come from the head, others the feet, while dirt used in love spells is supposed to be taken from the heart. You can take your pick, as this is just another reason to gather your own graveyard dirt! In collecting the dirt you should pay the spirit in the grave for it.

Graveyard dirt may have other things added to it, to complete the spell such as herbs, feathers, snakeskin, or powdered bones. In the initiatory African Palo practice it is considered to be a very powerful material indeed. The Palero usually connects the spirit of a dead person to the graveyard dust they use.

G

Those who regularly work with the dead will have much better luck using graveyard dirt than those who are unfamiliar with such work. If you are new to working with the dead, it might pay to ask someone more experienced for some assistance.

GRINDELIA   (Grindelia Robusta [#1103] or Camporum [?]) Gum Plant   An expectorant and sedative as well as being excellent for the treatment of bronchial problems. Once used in treating Asthma.

GROUND PINE (Lycopodium Complantatum) [#1404]   A stimulant and diuretic. It strengthens the nerves and relieves aches and pains. Good in the treatment of rheumatism and female complaints. As it promotes menstruation, pregnant women should never take it.

GUARANA (Paullinia Sorbilis) [#1674]   The extract of the seed is used, it is a nervine, a tonic, a slightly narcotic stimulant, and supposedly, an aphrodisiac. It is excellent in treating nervous headaches and fatigue. (var. is P. Cupana)

GUAR GUM   Used to promote weight loss.   The gum supposedly swells in the stomach to give a feeling of fullness. It is not recommended for this use.

Guar gum is also used as a mucilaginous agent, in mixtures of various kinds, such as Pembas, baths, and spells. It may be added to various magical body powders as a strong tea, and mixed into the powder well. The paste mixture is dried and reground. This will make the powders adhere to the body better.

GULTA   A region on the North Carolina Atlantic Ocean Seacoast which developed an African American 'root working' practice all its own. This area also produced the 'cake walk dance,' as African Americans were forbidden to dance rapidly there. Thus their dance pattern became a kind of shuffle. One of the more interesting places in America to visit.

H

HAITIAN OILS   Most of these oils, powders, and other such ingredients do not come from Haiti. They have only received that name because of the reputation of Haiti as a "Magic Island." Haitian Gamblers Oil for example is often just Red Palm Oil, often used as an anointing oil to end a streak of bad luck. A Haitian Hougon whom I spoke with had never heard of using it in this way, although he was familiar with red palm oil, which he used in cooking.

HAPPY TIMES POWDER   A casting powder spread around a room in order to lighten the vibration and eliminate depression. It can change the luck influence in a room, and open up a more positive money flow. The room must be first physically and non-physically cleaned to allow the lighter influence of this powder to linger.

> Cardamom Seed ¼ ounce
> Coriander Seed ¼ ounce
> Ginger Powder ¼ ounce
> Cinnamon Powder ¼ ounce

Grind the seeds to a powder in the mortar, and then sift the mixture several times to blend the mixture together. Once mixed, add one ounce of Lotus root powder to the mixture and mix again thoroughly. Let the mixture rest and blend for at least a week or two before use. Cast the powder throughout the room. It's beneficial for heartbreaks, romantic or otherwise.

HAWTHORN BERRIES [Crataegus Coccinea] [#771] {Crataegus Oxycantha} Used as a tonic for the heart. The tea of the bark and leaves is also used in a floor wash, to purify the ritual area before some kinds of ritual work. The tea is used to purfy homes as a floor and wall wash. It has a good effect. The berries are edible.

HAS HANNA (Tiene Hanna) A gardenia essential oil based product used to hold a mate. Gardenia essential oil adced to talc makes an effective powder for this purpose.

HAZELNUT (Corydalis Avellana [#761]or Corylus Americana [#760]) The Celtic nut of wisdom. Those who desire mental stability, calm, or insight into difficulties may use it. This is particularly beneficial for working with mundane worldly conditions, rather than theoretical or intellectual corditions of any kind. The meat of the nut is dried and ground into a fine powder.

HEAD WASHING COMPOUND In the Voudon religious practice part of the initiation is a formal head washing, which is done to clear away all obscurity from the person whose head is being washed. Many other practices have the same format, although washing the head is not always done as a part of the initiation ritual. The following head washing blend may be used in head washings, to clear a person's mentation. The difference from the initiatory head washing is the intent, and what other events precede and follows this head washing. This is not an initiation head washing.

> 1 teaspoon crushed Fenugreek seed
> 1/2 teaspoon Cinnamon powder
> 1 Oz. bunch of fresh Watercress, torn apart
> 1 Oz. bunch of fresh leafy (Italian) Parsley, torn
>   apart
> 1 Oz. bunch of fresh Regular Parsley, torn apart
> 1 Oz. bunch of fresh Basil, torn apart

H

7 small Garlic Cloves, crushed
1 Oz. bunch of fresh Coriander herb, torn apart.

Add the above to a gallon of river water, and let set in the sun for between 72 hours to a week. As the person's head is being washed the person doing the washing should pray for the person's spiritual elevation and mental clarity.

HEAL ALL (Collinsonoia Canadensis) [#690] Also called Stone Root, and Self Heal, it is a stimulant and a good general tonic. It is also said to strengthen the heart, aid the memory, and clear away minor complaints. Used to improve the memory and clear the mind. The leaves are a vulnary.

Also Prunella Vulgaris [#1828] (Prunella Officinalis) Self Heal The plant is an astringent, but I have not found it as useful as the one above.

Also Valeriana Officinalis [#2388] Valerian All Heal The Heal All Herb As a tea it will improve the general health.

HEALING OIL Powder (Curando) Carnation essential oil in perfume oil diluent is particularly useful for nurses, as it keeps them from attracting any miasma of disease. The presence of carnations in the sick room has a cleansing effect, as does the use of carnation scented talc on the patient.

HEALTH OIL Usually a green colored mineral oil used to anoint candles used for healing prayers. It should have a carnation scent.

HEARTSEASE (Viola Tricolor) [#2436] Pansy The plant is said to be a good general preventative for convulsions. It relieves congestion and has a mild laxative action. Ruled by Saturn, it is used in some love spells as a binder of the affections.

HEATHER Herb & Flowers (Erica Vulgaris) [#917] The plant is used as a charm, the flowers as an incense.

HEATHER OIL (BREZO) Heather blossoms or flowers are soaked in Sunflower seed oil for several weeks. The resulting oil has a nice perfume, and is used for vitalizing, as well as general massage and healing purposes.

HEAVY THOUGHT FORM ELIMINATOR   An incense made of equal parts of finely ground coffee, garlic powder, and brown sugar. Burned on charcoal to get rid of heavy thought forms and depressing vibrations in the place where it is burned. Good for homes that are full of argument, to rid the place of the vibration of heavy emotion, depression, and sadness that remains.

HELLBORE   American, White   (Veratrum Viride) [#2398] Also called Indian Poke Weed   It is a narcotic sedative, but as it brings on the menses, it should never be taken by pregnant women.

HELLBORE, Black   (Helleborous Niger)   [#1137]   The root is a poison, a strong sedative, and sometimes was used in the witches 'flying ointment' of the middle ages.

HELL'S DELIGHT   A Hexing oil used in laying strong curses. It is made from nine parts of ebony wood powder, one half-part gunpowder, three parts graveyard dirt, then mixed with as much mineral oil as desired. It should be thick, but not so thick as to become a stiff paste. Black candles are dressed with this oil and burned to cause the victim harm. Use this oil with great caution, as the work can rebound on you.

HELONIAS   Root   (Helonias Dioica)   [#1139]   Also known as Star Root, or False Unicorn Root   Used in Root working as a power root.

HENBANE   (Hyoscyamus Niger)   [#1186]   The herb is a poisonous narcotic. It can cause insanity and should never be taken internally.   Useful medically in some nervous and irritability conditions, it can alter the state of consciousness, even destroying the mentation. An excellent sedative but great caution must be exercised when working with it. Henbane was used in the witches flying ointment of the middle ages, a very good reason not to use it.

H

HENNA   [Lawsonia Intermis]   [#1314]   Used for hair care since Egyptian times, when it was the foremost hair care product in the Mediterranean world.   It is the ground or powdered leaf of a shrub like plant that grows in the Middle East.   Henna is famed for its ability as a dye.   Used for the protection of mediums, a bowl of water with a pinch of henna in it may be used as protection in séances.

Because of its power, Henna is an ingredient in five element charms.   A henna bath will restore psychic equilibrium, but the quantity of Henna must be sufficient that its dye action is not over much for the person who is bathing.   It is infrequently used in magic as an incense.   Adds stability to most incenses, when used in very small quantities.   Henna is often combined with powdered ginger for enhancing the effect of incenses.

Henna is available in many varieties today; it should be used for hair care first, as it is not a great general-purpose incense. The ground root powder is a better incense, but it is the juice that is used as a dyestuff.   Used internally and externally for afflictions of the skin.

Henna works well as a magical powder.   It will accept a charge without difficulty, and it may be mixed with other powders as desired.   It will act to influence thoughts, but not as strongly as High John the Conqueror.

The magical effect of Henna, which has been used cosmetically since prehistoric times, was one of the reasons why hair dressing was considered a sacred occupation, and was reserved for priestesses, or women who were candidates for the priesthood.

Some people are sensitive to Henna, and it can cause rather than remedy skin disorders.

HEMLOCK   The drink that killed Socrates?   Not from the North American Hemlock tree.   [Abies Canadensis   #4]   The Hemlock Spruce.   This tree has leaves that may be used to produce an abortive tea, and a bark useful in tanning leather. It also produces a useful pitch or gum resin.

American Hemlock is useful for taming enemies, if you write the enemies name on a piece of paper and tie it to some of the tree bark. Now pray over the combination, and keep the bark and name hidden in a dark and damp place, to place a spell on the one named on the paper.

The fatal hemlock, Conium Maculatum [#703] is a poison narcotic sedative and anodyne. It was once used in spasmodic or nervous conditions. An overdose produces paralysis and death. It was another toxic substance supposedly used in the occasionally fatal witches flying ointments of the middle ages.

Water Hemlock, Cicuta Douglasi, [# ?], or Cicuta Virosa, [#614] {Var. Cicuta Maculata}, in its European version, was supposedly another ingredient in these flying ointments. Another herb should never be taken internally, as it causes death in a matter of minutes.

HEXING   Hexing is jinxing, or putting a curse on someone. There are no special Hex products that are not also Jinx or Curse or even Mojo products. Hex refers to witch in German. Thus a Hexenmeister is a 'witch master,' or someone who can undo the spells cast by a witch.

HIGH ALTAR   (Altar Mayor) (Altar Alto) Used to attract good spirits to a blessed altar. The oil is made with olive oil, benzoin, camphor, frankincense, and myrrh. For the best effect allow it to sit for a month, shaking occasionally, before using.

The best incense for this purpose is Church Incense with half as much extra Benzoin added to it.

HIGH ALTAR POWDER   The powder is sprinkled on an altar to attract spirits to assist in or enhance the work being done. Another powder for this purpose is Drawing Powder used to draw a spirits of the dead for any purpose. These are both summoning powders.

In practice, the nature of a summoning powder must change with kind of spirits you wish to work with. The following two powders will summon all kinds of spirits.

HIGH SPIRIT SUMMONING POWDER
Equal parts of white eggshell powder and Lotus root.

H

LOW SPIRIT SUMMONING POWDER

Equal parts of Sulfur and Asafetida

The powders should not be mixed, and the altar should be well cleaned between using the two powders.

HIGH JOHN THE CONQUEROR   [Ipomaea Jalapa] [#1225]   (Jalap)   (Juan El Conquistador)   The most popular of all of the Gulta root worker and Hoodoo roots. It is carried as a charm, and is supposed to draw love. It is also carried for gambling luck, good health, and for money. Used as a major ingredient in many root-working spells, it is one of the principle controlling, or commanding, herbs known. Medically, it is an energetic laxative, and must be used with great care.

When carried whole, it is usually kept in a red charm bag. It may be added to a special oil, which is to be rubbed on the hands before gambling. The oil is usually plain mineral oil with some colorant in it, in which pieces of the root have been kept a week or so, usually while exposed to the sunlight.

High John the Conqueror may be made into a water, oil, or ground into a powder, but it is always used for controlling either people or situations. The root often forms part of the Lucky Hand Charm, carried to attract good fortune.

The powder is rubbed on the hands for gambling, and on the body for blessings and protection. It is a useful money powder, and the most useful of all of the commanding powders.

HINDU GRASS OIL   Lemon grass in either olive, or more likely, mineral oil. The oil is used for protection. In India, it is made from Lemon grass, while the oil is often kerosene.

HINDU OIL   Usually Van Van Oil. Used for Good luck.

HOG GUM   Palo Conchino   Astragalus Tragacan- [#318] The twigs are made into a Palo. The gum is an incense of dubious quality, but it is a viscous and useful gum.

HOLY HERB   Pure European Vervain herb. This herb is used as an incense, a bath ingredient, a tea, and a sprinkle.

Known as "Enchanters Herb" it has a very great number of uses in all kinds of magic. A bath of the herb is an excellent curse breaker.

HOLY POWDER

This powder is used to prevent evil spirits from blocking a person's path in life. It is a soothing and healing powder, and has a mildly elevating effect on most people. As a blow powder, it may be applied to a person after a spiritual cleansing.

Two sticks of white chalk ground to a
fine powder
One teaspoon of finely ground eggshell powder
One teaspoon of arrowroot powder
A few grains of salt

Sift together several times. It is then ready for use either as a blow powder or a casting powder.

HOLY SPIRIT POWDER One of the most beneficial powders, it s sprinkled to draw beneficial spirits to aid an individual in their spiritual evolution. The powder may be used as desired, including being burned as incense.

Benzoin Powder – 1 ounce
Myrrh Powder – ½ ounce
Sandalwood Powder – ¼ ounce

Mix well and store in an amber bottle. Sprinkle on the altar, the bedroom, between the bed sheets, or burn as an incense.

HOLY THISTLE (Centaurea Benedicta) [#558] {Chicus Benedictus} Blessed Thistle. A protective tea is made from the herb and sprinkled around the outside of the house. It is also useful in blessing people.

Steeping the herb in Olive Oil for several weeks makes the Oil.

HONEY (Miel) Books have been written about the medicinal and magical uses of honey. It is the one food that cannot spoil, as it is antiseptic and will not support the growth of bacteria. Potassium deficiencies may be corrected by

H

drinking a teaspoon of apple cider vinegar and two teaspoons of honey in a glass of warm water. This drink also good for reducing the mucous in the throat. Honey is better used for cooking than white sugar.

A useful floor wash may be made from a teaspoon of honey to a gallon of water. Dissolve the Honey in the water. This wash is used to wash away the effects of a curse or negativity after the cleansing has taken place. It is good wash to use on the front steps of a house, to attract beneficial influences into the home.

HONEYSUCKLE (Madreselva) The plant is good to have in the garden, especially along fences. The power and perfume made from the essential oil are best used for business places to draw money to a person or place of business. The oil, made from the flowers, is a mental stimulant.

HOPS Flowers [Humulus Lupulus] [#1169] Used in making beer, it has a calming effect when used as a herb in baths. The tea of the flowers is usually added to other bath mixtures, but it may be used by itself. It may also be burned as incense, but hops are usually more effective when used in a bath or sprinkle. A herb of Mars, it is used to induce sleep, when the flowers are placed in a pillow. Used medicinally in former times, it is now used only in making beer. Anti aphrodisiac, it is a relaxant and sedative hypnotic that often produces sleep. Sleeping on a pillow stuffed with hops will encourage a deep sleep. It can even cause a mental stupor. The tea should not be taken internally.

HOREHOUND [Marrubium Vulgare] [#1428] It is to be kept near the doorway of a home to keep troubles of all kinds away. A good general floor rinse if you can get it fresh, or find it growing near your home.

A hand full of leaves make the tea, and added to three gallons of water, it makes a good floor wash for placing generally good vibes into the home.

HORSEBANE (Oenathe Phellandrium) [#1595] A Water Hemlock. A narcotic and often toxic herb that should be used very carefully, if at all.

HORSE CHESTNUT [#75] See Buckeye See Chestnut - Used to adsorb pain of arthritis, or rheumatism, which it does with a certain degree of effectiveness. The nut is often carried by those who have arthritis or rheumatism. When the skin of the nut cracks, the nut should be discarded.

Ideally, the nut should be prayed over for this purpose before it is given to the person who is to use it. A bowl of these nuts may be used in the sick room to assist with reducing pain. They should be washed in cool water every day to extend their ability to adsorb pain. Also see Buckeye and Chestnut.

HORSENETTLE (Solanum Carolinense) [#2177] An excellent narcotic nervine, which was once found good for menstrual problems.

HORSE RADISH Rabano picante (Cochleria armorica L.) [#680] The shredded white root stem of the plant is used as a cordiment. The chopped new leaves are used as a garnish in salads when fresh in the summer. Used to heat up spells in which the emotions are a factor. Not very favorable for love spells, better for lust spells. Best used for spells where anger, lust, and other strong emotions are to be aroused.

HORSETAIL GRASS (Erigeron Canadense) [#919] Also known as Shave Grass, it is used as a healing tea for its silica content. A better remedy is to use gelatin, even in the form of the sweetened desert product. The two have about the same effect in strengthening the nails, cartilage, and the horned tissue of the body.

HOT FOOT POWDER Used to lay minor curses, it has the effect of giving the enemy a "Hot Foot." It may be used as a blow powder, or it may be applied directly to the body of the person to be cursed, or to their trace. The mixed powder must sit seven days before being used, and prayed over both while being mixed, and for each specific use.

H

The powder is made of one Tablespoon of Hot Chili Powder, One Tablespoon of Mustard Powder, One Tablespoon of Iron filings, One Tablespoon of Patchouli Herb Powder, and One Tablespoon of Ground Musk Root.

A considerably less complicated mixture is made from pure red pepper powder. It is placed on a trace of the enemy and prayed over for the effect desired. It does not last long, and is not harmful to the person, but it will make them uncomfortable.

Another blend of Hot Foot Powder uses red pepper, black pepper, and powdered sulfur. As with many of these formulas, there are any numbers of them to choose from. Take your pick.

HOUSE BLESSING INCENSE (Benediction del Hogar) Made of Myrtle, Camphor, and Nutmeg, this incense is used to fumigate the home. This is done before, or along with, any other work done to bless and protect the home.

For example, the windows and doors might be sealed with Holy Oil, but the house should be fumigated with House Blessing Incense first. This incense seals and protects the house from evil influences.

HOUSE DRESSING POWDER A corner powder that is to be placed in all of the corners of the house. Discouraging to negative entities, it adds blessing and protection to the house, making people feel more at ease, and more at home.

This powder is made from a quarter ounce of Camphor, an ounce of Myrtle leaves well powdered, and an ounce of powdered Aloe Vera. Pray over it before use and put a pinch of the powder in all of the many corners of the house.

ANOTHER HOUSE DRESSING POWDER Used to bless a house or apartment and prepare it for occupancy. Use in a physically clean but unoccupied dwelling. For an occupied dwelling, see Happy Times Powder.

    Myrtle leaves, powdered - ½ ounce
    Cascarilla bark, ground - 1 ounce
    Lucky Hand root, powdered - 2 ounces

113

Powdered white eggshell – 1/2 ounce

Mix well and pray over it for divine blessings on the home where it is to be used. Sprinkle throughout the dwelling. Not a house cleaner, but a good house blessing powder.

HOUSE LEEK Siempre Viva, or Prodigisa Semprivum Tectorum [#2108] Ruled by Jupiter, Domain of Chango. The living plant is used in marriage spells, as the plant grows so does the marriage or the relationship. Medically, it is an astringent vulnary.

HUCKLEBERRY Whortleberry [Vaccinium Myrtillus] [#2377] The berries are used as a dye, as well as for bird feed. Make a tea of the sun-dried berries, and sprinkle it around the premises to free the home from depression.

The dried berries are good to keep in the sick room to fight despair, hopelessness, and depression, in the patient. The leaves are burned in the bedroom before sleep, to promote true dreaming.

HUMAN MILK Used to promote marriages, as in the two milks charm, where the milk from a mother and daughter are used for this purpose. The different milks regularly consumed by humans include that of the buffalo, camel, cow, goat, horse, sheep, and reindeer. They all have different qualities.

HYDROPHILIA (Hydrophilia Spinosa) [NONE] A demulcent and diuretic. Often considered an aphrodisiac, I know not why.

HYSSOP [Hyssopus Officinalis] [#1197] Ruled by Jupter in Cancer, it is the sacred herb of Judaism, and is used in spiritual cleansing, baths, and sprinkles. These baths are especially useful for Jewish people who are confused about their religious place, or their religion. A blood regulator, it decreases the blood pressure, increasing the circulation. Medically, it has been used to kill body lice and help break up mucus in the lungs and throat. It also expels worms. A decoction of the herb can be used to remove the discoloration from black eyes.

H

From ancient times Hyssop has been used as an aspergillium for other sprinkles. The plant itself is used for protection against the evil eye. A sprig of hyssop is said to repel evil from wherever it is hung. The tea in a bath is purifying and removes negative influences. The herb will also cut the grease of fatty dishes served at the table. Thus it is good to serve with roast duck or roast lamb.

Hyssop tea dispels bad vibes when sprinkled around the home, or used as a floor wash. Taken internally, the tea is said to excite the passions. A tea of the herb is often used in purification, or lustral baths, taken before doing certain ritual work. It is often used in exorcisms and purification.

See Psalms 51:7, Exodus 12:22, John 19:29, and Hebrews 9:19, for biblical references to Hyssop.

I

IGNATIUS BEANS   (Strychnos Ignatia)   [#2234]   The seed is a bitter, poisonous, bean. Medically it has been used as a stimulant, and in the treatment of nervous disorders. It is best used medically in the Homeopathic dilution. The bean may be used as a protective charm, and can be made into a protective necklace for this purpose.

INDIAN ARROWOOD   Same as Wahoo Bark, which see.

INDIAN BALM   Same as Beth Root, which see.

INDIAN HEMP, BLACK   (Apocynum Canabium)   [#219] A Bitter tasting diuretic. It is not a narcotic.

INDIAN HEMP, FOREIGN   (Cannabis Indica)   [#486] The extract is a Narcotic, antispasmodic, anodyne.

COMMON HEMP   (Cannabis Sativa)   [NONE]   Narcotic, used as above, do not confuse with Brazilian Jaborandi Root (Pi ocorpus Selloanus)   [NONE] which is also called Indian Hemp. It is a non-narcotic stimulant.

I

INDIAN INCENSE   American Indians, or Native Americans are said to have used Sage as their primary cleansing incense. Bundles of sage for smudging are available for this purpose.

INDIAN TOBACCO INCENSE   (Tobaco Di Indio)   The commercial incense often has little or no Tobacco in it.   Plain Tobacco, crumbled from a cigar, or from a tobacco hand, is more suitable for the purpose.   The fumes have a protective martial vibration.

INDIGO ROOT   Anil   Indigofera Anil   [#1217]   The source of Indigo dye, which comes from the root and leaves. The dye is used as an astral strengthener, to build strength in the aura of the people who bathe in it.   The root will take and hold a magical charge with great clarity, so some of the root powder may be added to spells, to make their charge stronger. The dye strengthens the astral fabric.   Best used as a soaking bath or wash.
Also see Baptisia Tinctoria   #349   Wild Indigo Plant.

INSTIGATION POWDER   A powder used to make people work.   A bit difficult to make and tricky to use, but it usually exceeds all expectations.   The effects last from several weeks to several months when used in the workplace or the home.   It acts as a sort of non-physical pick me up.   This powder is to be put in place shortly after the new Moon.

Hyssop Powder – 1 ounce
Rue Powder – 1 ounce
Verbena powder 3 ounces
Clove spice powder – 1 ounce
Galangal powder – 2 ounces
Finest Grind Coffee – 1 ounce

Sift the powder together several times to mix it well, tighten set it aside in a closed container, to blend for several days.

To use, burn some of the powder as an incense, and place a pinch in each corner of the room.

IRIS (Iris Florentina) [#1232] The Greek messenger of the Gods, the plant named after her is the source of Orris root, used in communications with the non-physical realms. (See Orris) Iris Powder is powdered Orris Root, and is used in blessing and protection work.

IRIS PERFUME OIL is made with Orris Root powder and Iris scent in a perfume base. It increases determination, communication, and concentration. Good for wearing on the temples in meditation, especially for beginners at meditation.

IRISH MOSS (Chondrus Crispus) [#606] Also called Pearl Moss - or Carragreen A nutrient, it has been used to control diarrhea, as well as being a cough remedy. It is considered a good luck plant; it is often placed about the house, and under the carpets, to attract good luck and good fortune to the home.

IRON FILINGS Used to feed the Lodestone, this material may be purchased by the pound from scientific supply houses. Also known as Magnetic Sand, or Lodestone food, which see.

IRON WEED (Veronia Fasciculata, (Var. Veronia Angustifolia)) [#2408] The root is used as a bitter tonic. It is used magically to restore peace and harmony to a home, or to a place that has been troubled, especially one that has been troubled by spirits. If it is prepared in a purple charm bag, it will be useful to assist in controlling others.

IVY [Hedera Helix] [#1122] A female plant, as contrasted with Holly, as a male plant. It is somewhat poisonous, but was used in medicine for many years non-the less.

The berries, known as Issue Peas, are an emetic and cathartic. The leaves are a stimulant and vulnary. The decoction tea of the leaves attacks the mentation, and can drive those who ingest it into a furry of madness. The herb is used magically as a protection against evil. The tea is also used to make people mad when applied to a trace or image of the victim, but with variable success.

J

JABORANDI   (Piper Reticulatum)   [#1739] (Later: Filocarpus Jaborandi)   An antidote for atropine. Useful for Psoriasis, and some types of deafness. The infusion is made with one oz of leaves to one pt. of boiling water. The dose is said to be a wineglass full, (two Oz.) or less, as needed.

JALAP Root   Jalop Root   See High John the Conqueror. Jalap powder is the powdered root.

JAMAICA BUSH POWDER   Used to bring luck while either gambling or investing.   Made from undiluted Jamaica bark powder, or Cinchona.
The Water, Jamaica Bush Water, is a tea of the powder used in baths for the same purpose.

JAMAICA GINGER WATER   Steep about a cup of ginger sliced into quarter thick pieces in a gallon of boiling water. Allow the water to come to room temperature. The water may be used as an expediter to be added to baths and floor washes, about an ounce for baths and two or three ounces for floor washes. It may also be used as a wash or a bath for people who have the chills.

JAPANESE OIL JAPAN OIL (Japones)   Japan Oil is an article of commerce used in the paint industry. As volatile oil, it is used in dissipating negative spiritual forces. Rubbing alcohol works as well, and is easier to find. The more volatile oils and fluids, such as Alcohol, Acetone, and Paint Thinner (Mineral spirits), and so on must be handled with great care as they are a serious fire hazard.

JASMINE Flowers   [Jasminum Officinale]   [#1246] {Jasminum Odoratissimum} The oil is used as a calmative in a place where there is excess nervous energy, or mental tension. Add to love spells, and to baths, to calm excited or nervous people. A good relaxing bath when used by itself. Add to love incense when the person is nervous about doing the spell.

The tea of the flowers, or the extracted oil is used. Yellow Jasmine   (Gelsensium Sempervirens [#1043]) is used as a calmative, but an overdose causes convulsions and gives symptoms of toxicity.

JERICHO Flowers (?) (The Resurrection Plant) Used as a charm in the home or place of business.

JERUSALEM OAK (Chenopodium Anthelminticum) [#591] The fruit of this tree yields the Oil of Worm Seed. Used for hex and spell casting to annoy enemies.

JEZEBEL ROOT [# ?] Used in spells of influence and binding. A controlling powder. It should be held in the hand while cursing your enemy. Then place it in a jar half full of warm water, close the jar and put it away for three days. Throw the jar in a river while cursing your enemy again.

The water is made by boiling the root, and is used in a bath by women who wish to seduce a specific man.

JIMSON WEED [Datura Stramonium] [#845] A narcotic poisonous hallucinogenic weed.   Ruled by Jupiter, the dried leaves are sprinkled to hide a trail, to conceal something, or to hide someone.   Medically, the fumes have been used for treating asthma. This treatment is not recommended.

J

JINX REMOVING BATH (Remueve lo Malo, or Arasa con Todo) The best material for a curse or jinx breaking bath is Mate herb tea. Place a cup of the tea in a tub half full of water and stay in the tub for six or eight minutes. Air dry on leaving the tub.

JINX REMOVING FLOOR WASH   Mate herb tea, as mentioned above, may be used diluted a cup of the tea to three gallon bucket of floor wash water.

Another jinx removing floor wash is made from equal parts of Yarrow herb and Aloe Vera. In some cases a perfume is added. This blend may also be used as an incense. It is a useful floor wash to remove the miasma of an illness from a place.

JINX REMOVING INCENSE   Burned to ward off and protect from Jinxes, Hexes, and Curses, it is made from so called musk crystals. This material is often made available in a variety of colors, supposedly for different things. It is usually about 90% colored filler power, and about 10% so-called musk crystals.

JINX REMOVING POWDER   (Inside-Outside Powder) Usually used to protect against jinxes, or hexes. Placed around the walls of the house, the powder is usually made from powdered Winter's Bark herb, or wood four, with a martial perfume and red coloring added to it.

JOB   (Trabajo)   Van-van oil is used to help people find work. It should be prayed over for the person, not for the job they want. The person applies it to their temples and sternum when they go out looking for work.

JOB BREAKER   (Quebra Trabajo)   Used to make people lose their jobs, it is made from red (Capsicum) pepper in Van van oil. This also must be prayed over for the person, not for the job.

JOBS TEARS [Coix Lachryma] [#686] Carried for luck. Seven of the tears (seeds) are to be carried in the pocket for luck and general good fortune. For a specific wish, think clearly of what you wish, holding the seven seeds in the palm of your hand. Place the seeds in a charm bag one at a time. Then carry the bag with you for seven days, and your wish should come true.

JOCKEY CLUB POWDER Used as a hex breaker, it actually takes its name from a very popular perfume line in the 1890's. Herewith the original 1892 formula for Jockey Club Perfume Oil, for use by men, as published in a "Handy Book Of Useful Formulas."

> Extract Jasmin – 5 ounces
> Extract Orris – 20 Ounces
> Extract Musk – 7 ounces
> Extract Vanilla – 1 ½ Ounces
> Otto Rose, virgin – 1 ½ drams
> Otto Santal f. lav. – 1 ½ drams
> Otto Neroli, super – 40 minimums
> Benzoic Acid - 2 drams
> Pure Spirit (Ethyl alcohol) – to make 4 pints

This is another example of the practitioner using what is at hand at the time to do what has to be done. This is the real essence of practical magical operations.

JOHN'S BREAD Carob St Johns Bread (Ceratonia Siliqua) [#574] The pods are used, they are highly nutritional for both man and beast. Used by singers for the improvement of their voice.

JOY POWDER Another sexual stimulant and attraction powder. Usually prepared as a body powder, with the perfumes added and blended for the effect desired. Made of powdered dry pink rose petals, lilac, sweet pea oil, and musk, in a talc base.

JU-JU Oil, Powder, Incense, etc. JuJu is a western African word covering all forms of magic, or psychic, practices.

J

There is no specific product for this purpose. This phrase could be used to cover all of the products in these pages.

JULA METZA POWDER   This powder is made under the influence of a voudon Loa, under ritual conditions. It is not likely to be found in an occult store. It is used as an uncrossing powder, to remove curses from someone. Ideally, it is used by a medium passing the Loa at a time.

JUM-JUM-JUM POWDER   A blend used to calm the mind and relieve mental anguish.   Before using the powder, the cause of mental anguish should be looked into and alleviated if possible.

> Powdered Jasmine Leaves – 2 ounces
> Powdered Sunflower petals – 2 ounces
> Powdered Orrisroot – 1 ounce

Mix well and sift together several times.   Use a blow powder, blow on the person.   In extreme cases, it may be rubbed on the head.   It is an effective powder for most cases of anguish and mental distress.

JUNIPER BERRIES   [Juniperus Communis] [#1257]   The berries are a mild diuretic, little used.   May be steeped in wine, and the wine taken daily for increasing the vitality.   Used to increase male sexual potency, the berries are added to red wine and allowed to stand for several weeks.   A wineglass full every night is the dose. (2 Oz) As a tea, it is beneficially used for the eyes, as an aid to the memory, and for the brain.   The ground berries are occasionally used as incense.

JUPI POWDER   A crossing powder, cast to lay curses on enemies, it is often said to be the same as Jua-Jua powder.   It is made from "Jumby Beans," which are crushed in the name of the person who is to be cursed.   It causes argument and dissension, usually making the cursed person quarrel with their friends and leave their family.   It is very effective against enemies.

JUPITER POWDER   Used in efforts suitable to the planetary spirit of Jupiter, usually in rituals performed on Thursday.   Made of equal parts of Cinnamon, Clove, and Nutmeg. This may also be used as a money powder, or as an incense.

JURY WINNING POWDER   See John the Conquer Powder, which is the same thing. Used to help win court cases, it is sprinkled in the jury box and on the judge's seat.

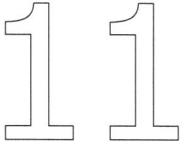

K

KABALA POWDER   An attraction powder used in solitary communion with spirits.   This powder must be used only in solitude, as it is not suitable for group ceremonies.   Used while burning a white candle.   The powder is made of Wisteria and Oak Moss powders.   This powder has nothing at all to do with the Jewish mystical Kabbalah.   It had been named this only to give it some sort of authenticity.

KANANGA   [Cananga Odorata] Ylang Ylang, which see.

KAVA KAVA ROOT   [Piper Methysticum]   [#1736]   The root is said to make an aphrodisiac tea when soaked in hot water.   As it is also used in treating gout, this use is quite doubtful.   Also said to be a general protection against harm, and to bring good luck if carried.   Smells like lilac, it is often used in love charms and sachets.

KEEP AWAY EVIL (Contra Lo Malo) Incense Frankincense and Benzoin, which have been aged together for three months make an excellent banishing incense for this purpose.   Fumigate the person who has the problem, and allow them to adsorb the fumes of the incense into their aura.

KELP   (Fucus Versiculosus)   [#1017]   Sea Wack, when burned in the open air becomes Kelp.   Used in food for its iodine content.   Formerly used in rush beds, particularly in Ireland, supposedly to keep the sleeper from being psychically attacked at night.

KHUS KHUS   [Andropogon Muricatus]   Vettivert   [#178] Kus Kus   The root is used to make the perfume. It is famous in the West Indies, where it is a popular charm. As a charm, the root is carried in a red charm bag for love, luck, and general success.

Used in incense for its sandalwood like odor. The cold soaking tea is said to attract benevolent spirits when it is put in the bath water. The essence used for the tea is extracted by soaking in cold water for three days or more. This root apparently should not be boiled.

KINDLY SPIRIT POWDER   Makes people feel sympathy for you and like you.   Use in any ritual where you wish to overcome loneliness or gain a friendly shoulder to cry on. Made of Mace and Narcissus, with talc.   Good for those who are overcome with self-pity.

KISS ME QUICK   A party powder, worn when a one night stand or a quick romance is desired.   Cherry blossoms for confidence, Rose Germanium oil for romance, Orrisroot powder for communications, and a bit of Myrrh to bring the desires to Manifestation. Age the mixture for at least two weeks, and add unscented Talc. Again, age for a month or so before use.

KNOT WEED   (Polygonum Persicaria)   [#178]   Knot Grass   Antiseptic, good for the treatment of cuts and bruises. A vulnary. Magically, it is used in binding spells and rituals.

Used in Bruno's curse, where a doll made with the herb stuffed or placed inside, and the name of the enemy pinned to it on the outside is beaten with a stick while the following is said:

> "With this stick I beat you, and break you, and curse you.   Oh Great Bruno, help me to rid myself of this person and the thought of him."

K

Then bury the doll on a Friday night, and leave without looking back at it's grave. (And just who is Bruno?)

KOLA (Cola Acuminata) [#687] Cola Nut Kola Nut A stimulant, tonic, and nervine. Contains caffeine, and makes a good substitute for coffee. Used in making Cola drinks.

The nuts are used in divination in several African divination systems.

KUMARHOU (Pomaderris Elliptica) [?] A general tonic and blood purifier. It is also good for the treatment of asthma, bronchitis and rheumatism. The infusion is made of a half Oz. of the herb to One pt. of boiling water. Dose is a wineglass full (Two ounces) each day.

KYOTO POWDER A powder used on the head of a person who has had a run of bad luck or has just recovered from an illness. It is supposed to "Pick Up The Life," another name for the powder.

Made from crushed black tea, it s rubbed in the head and hair of the afflicted person, along with a prayer for their health and good fortune.

KYPHI Incense, Oil, Powder Made from the dried petals of the Carnation, Lotus, and Germanium flowers. These should be ground together and allowed to rest for at least a week. The ground petals are burned as the incense, added to Olive or Sunflower Oil to make the Oil, and to Talc to make the powder.

These products are used as a banishing incense. A bit of cinnamon added to the oil makes it suitable for placing on the cash register every day to draw money to a place of business.

L

LAD'S LOVE (Ledum Latifolium) [#261]   Southernwood, which see. It is an aromatic and astringent. Ruled by Mercury, it is used in the same way as wormwood, except that its scent is far more pleasant.

LADY LUCK POWDER A powder used to promote success at gambling, made of ground nutmeg. The formula is variable, but many people use only ground nutmeg, sometimes adding talc as filler. The following is an occult store formula:

> Powdered Nutmeg 2 Ounces
> Powdered Cinnamon ¼ Ounce
> Powdered Orrisroot 1 Ounce
> Powdered Sandalwood 1 Ounce
> Talcum Powder 4 To 8 Ounces

Sift together several times to mix well, put in a closed container after adding a drop of Jasmine perfume oil. Let the materials mix together for a week or two, shaking the container frequently, before using.

L

LADY'S MANTLE (Alchemilla Vulgaris) [#92] One of the best vulnaries, used for the treatment of wounds. An astringent, it stops bleeding and heals bruises, cuts, and inflammations. Infusion is One Oz. of the herb to One Pt. Boiling Water.

LADY'S SLIPPER Root (Cypripedium Pubescens) [#830] An antispasmodic, nervine, and tonic that calms, relieves pains, and aids sleep. It is good in the relief of female problems. The inner bark is used.   It is primarily a medical herb, known as the American Valerian. The tea is used as an anti Hysteric. Used for female complaints and hysteria. Taken in honey water. One drachm to One half pint of water.

Magically, it is used in baths, but to little effect.

LAUREL Leaves The kitchen Bay Leaf, which see. Given to brides to wear to promote a long and happy marriage. Rubbed on the joints to prevent arthritis, to some slight healing effect. A hallucinogen.

LAVA   The product of volcanic action, lava is another natural ingredient that has found a use in magical work. Lava that has erupted from a volcano and is collected as dust, usually far from the eruption, is used as a magical expediter. Lava that has flowed and stopped is used to bring things to a halt. The flowed lava is usually powdered for this purpose.

LAVENDER [Lavandula Vera] [#1311] {L Officinalis} Ruled by Mercury, tending more to Mercury in Virgo than Mercury in Gemini. Burned with incense to bring peace to the home. Also said to assist in obtaining love and money. The dried flowers are used in sachets pertaining to love and peace. A mild stimulant, it helps headaches and prevents fainting. Aromatic, the flowers are used in pillows, linen sachets, etc. where it has a distinctly feminine vibration.

In Victorian England it was used as a wishing charm. Lavender blossoms placed under the pillow, were supposedly an indication that the wish would come true if the person dreamed of their wish that night.

Induces trances when used as a smoking mixture. Sprinkled on the head to keep the person chaste. As a wash it is said to bring harmony to the home. As an incense, it will assist in dispelling strife and tension. A tea of the leaves is used for nausea and minor stomach upsets.

LEEK   Allium Porrum   [#104]   Vegetable food. The bulb is used in Welsh and Irish Magic as a poppet for healing. The Whole Leek is prayed over and 'worked' in the name of the person to be healed.

LEMON BALM   Leaves   (Melissa Officinalis)   [#1464] Balm   The flowers are used in perfume making. The leaves make a tea used in sponging off the sick to rid them of any miasma remaining from an illness.

LEMONGRASS   (Andropogon Citratum)   [#177]   The oil is used in perfumes, it is a stimulant to the system. Used to relieve indigestion, heartburn, and help in reducing fevers. Also used in any love perfume or oil desired, as it has a fragrance that takes and radiates the magical intent charged onto it.

LEMON   Whole, Peel, Spanish Oil   (Citrus Limonum) [#653]   Ruled by the Sun and Leo. The peel yields Oil of Lemon, used in perfumery. The whole lemon is used in magic, as well as its parts. A Lemon cut into four pieces is said to being bad luck on the person who cuts it. Lemons used in magic should always be cut either in half or in thirds. A drop or two of lemon juice in water makes a good eyewash. The Lemon is used to sour a person's life, all of the spells using this fruit are for bringing evil to others, or keeping them from doing evil to the spell worker.

To sour a life, cut into a lemon (Lengthwise) and place inside the name of the person whose life is to be soured, written on a piece of paper, folded in half with some red pepper placed inside the paper. Then wrap the lemon with black thread. Hold it in the icebox or freezer for seven days, then set it out where it will slowly rot.

L

LEMON VERBENA   Leaves   (Aloysia Triphylla)   [?]   Used in spell casting to increase the power of the spell. Add to rituals for help and success. May also be used to break up lovers, and marriages, by casting it on their doorstep at night. (Pray over it for the effect desired first). Can be used in baths to promote psychic opening.

LICORICE ROOT   Palo Dulce   [Glycyrrhiza Glabra] [#1077]   Ruled by Mercury Sweetwood   A perennial plant of the pea family, native to Europe. Helps soften people toward the one using it. Used in a variety of spells for this purpose. Used to calm nervous stomachs. It can be made into a tea, or the root itself may be chewed on. An ingredient of many love powders and potions. It may be sprinkled on the footprints of a lover to keep them faithful.

LIFE   EVERLASTING   (Gnaphalium   Polycephalum) [#1085]   {Also G_ Dioicum}   Flowers and Leaves   The White Balsam   A tea of this herb is supposed to preserve life if the following spell is spoken as it is drunk. "Chills and Ill, Pains and Banes, Do your fasting, and Life Everlasting."

This herb may be used to bring poverty on someone. A paper with their name and trace is wrapped around a twig of the weed. The paper is tied in place with three black ties and two red ties, alternating. It is then placed in the middle of a cross roads at midnight with the desired prayer.

LILLY   Flowers   All are ruled by the Moon. The Calla Lilly [#1948] is a symbol of resurrection. The Lilly of the Valley (Convallaria Majalis) [#707] (Ruled by Mercury and the Moon) is a symbol of purity and humility.   The Lilly is used for nervousness and heart trouble. It is a communicative perfume, encouraging relationships with others. The Day Lilly [#1140] is a symbol of coquetry. Some lily roots are used for treating gout, but other lily roots and flowers are poisonous.

LINDEN   [Tilia Americana [#2316] or Europaea [#2317] Lime   Keeps a lover faithful. Powder the bark or leaf and place a small dab of the powder on the beloved's forehead before retiring. Ruled by Jupiter.

131

Once used medically to reduce, or to stabilize, heart conditions. The flowers are a nervine, useful in calming the mind. In a bath, linden tea promotes perspiration, and is cooling to the head. It is used as a tonic for restlessness and headache.

LINSEED (Linseed Oil) [#1364] {Linum Usitatis simum} Burned in small quantities (A Drop or two on a hot charcoal) to attract divinatory powers. Make an equal limbed cross with the oil on each entrance to your home, and on all of your windows, to keep out evil spirits.

(? [Lippa Citriodora] (Aloysia Citriodora) [?] Reduces fever and (acts as a sedative. Taste and smell resemble lemon.)

LIRO BLANCO White Lilly, which see.

LOBELIA (Lobelia Inflata) [#1374] A nervine and an ant spasmodic of great value. Excellent in the relief of Bronchial problems and asthma.

LODESTONE The natural magnetic iron rock as supposedly first found in Magnesia, a province of Greece. The Locestones is used to draw things to someone, an example of sympathetic magic. In my own experience, I have found ceramic magnets to be at least as effective as natural lodestones. The use of the lodestone in magic is a field unto itself, as there are a number of folk spells using them. Locestones were considered live minerals by many natural philosophers until the Englishman Gilbert wrote about them as natural magnets in the early and mid 1600's.

PREPARING A MAGNETIC LODESTONE TO BE A
GUARDIAN OR PROTECTIVE SPIRIT
OF THE HOME

Take one lodestone, natural, not a painted one, and wash it in cold running water. Place the lodestone in a small glass container, something like a juice glass or the like. Hide it away in the dark place in the home where you will be keeping it for a day or so. Then take it out and place it in another glass. Feed it by pouring a shot or two of whiskey over it. Allow the lodestone to sit in the glass while you do the following.

Place symbols for some of the things you wish for in the house. For example, a silver dime for money, a (paper or plastic) heart for love, and so forth. Now place the lodestone back in it's glass home. Drink the remaining liquor in the second glass. Now sprinkle some 'magnetic sand' over the lodestone, about a half-teaspoon full is plenty. Replace the lodestone in its dark closet, and repeat the feeding ritual every week.

LODESTONE FOOD The Lodestone charm is fed with 'Magnetic Sand' which is actually a very finely powdered pulverized iron. This product is also known as iron filings, and is available from scientific supply houses by the pound. Fairly good for using in charm bags, but Red Ocher (FeO_2) is my first choice for charm bags. The Lodestone charm must be fed either with iron filings or with other powdered iron.

LODESTONE OIL (Piedra Iman) An attraction oil occasionally used to draw things to the user, or to break hexes and jinxes. It is made from magnetic sand or iron filings and mineral oil. A piece of lodestone is usually placed in the bottle. This oil must be exposed to the magnet, or magnetized, before it is used. I have found it to be ineffective for all but the weakest curses. However, it is quite popular.

LODESTONE POWDER A powder made from crushed lodestones, or from crushed Alnico or ceramic magnets. Used as a powder, it is added to some baths. It is also used as an attracting powder. A piece of lodestone – or a bit of powdered lodestone - is often put into the bottle of baths used to attract something to the user.

LODESTONE POWDER **LODESTONE FOOD** Iron filings, of the kind used to feed the lodestone used as a magical charm, a basic part of conjuring or folk magic practice. The finer these filings are, the better they work. The finest ones are quite useful in some other magical powders and charms. They may be purchased from machine shops or scientific supply stores.

The worst place to buy them is from an occult store.

See Magnetic sand. The best size of Lodestone powder is finer than ordinary sand.

LOST AND AWAY POWDER   Used to get rid of people you don't want around you. It gets them to move from their residence, or even to leave a job. It may either be put on the person, or placed on their doorstep.

This powder is made from: Deer Horn shavings, 5 to 10 parts.   Red Mercuric Oxide, (the Toxic Red precipitate of Mercury) 1 part,

LOVAGE   Root [Ligusticum Levisticum] [#1350]   The tea is used in a bath to assist the love life and to open the user, allowing them to become more sensitive to spiritual things. Ruled by the Sun in Taurus.

A bath of the ground root is supposed to open a person, and make them more loving, or to attract love to them. It is also supposed to be effective in winning court cases.

A marriage spell consists of splitting open a lovage root and placing a piece of paper with the names of the two lovers inside. The root is tied back in place with three threads, one white, one green, and one red. The packet is buried along the foundation wall of the house in which the two lovers live, or couple. The intention of this spell is to provide permanent love between the two people.

Used medically in the treatment of stomach disorders.

LOTUS   [Nelumbium Luteum]   [#1572]   Used in love spells, it is a symbol of human elevation and spiritual growth. Lotus seeds are used as a talisman, to insure good health and good fortune. They may be formed into a necklace for this purpose if desired.

Slices of the pod are used in divination. On a slice of Lotus root, yes is marked on one side, No on another. The root is tossed into the air, and the side showing once it comes down tells the answer to the question.

The stem and root are good fried and eaten, having an elevating effect on the person who eats it. The plant is water

134

grown, and therefore connected with the unconscious mind. It was a symbol of lower Egypt, but it has been used to represent deity throughout the world. The tubers are narcotic and poisonous.

The Lotus Flower is the Fleur de Lys, which later became the emblem of France. In a different stylization it was the symbol of lower Egypt, and of the Hindu deities as well.

LOTUS (Loto) Oil, Perfume, Incense, Powder All of these are usually made from the ground lotus root with Lotus essential oil used in the oil and perfume. The perfume often has some of the ground root in the bottle. Occasionally the powder of the dried Lotus flower is called for, which is more difficult to obtain.

These are all elevating and blessing products, and have a nice vibration. A Lotus bath may be made from Lotus root boiled in water. It has an elevating and clarifying effect on most people.

LOVE BREAKER OIL (Quebra Amor) Used to break up a love affair, or destroy a marriage. The person concerned may use this himself or herself if they desire. This may also be used to rid you of the undesired attentions of another person. The oil is put on a trace of one of the parties to the separation and prayed over for the effect desired.

The oil is made from sulfur and crushed mistletoe berries in mineral oil. It may be used as an anointing oil with a black candle to get rid of a mate, forcing them to leave you.

LOVE DRAWING (Atrayente de Amor) Sweet pea, an essential oil in a perfume diluent is better than anything else for attracting people to yourself. Once you meet the people you will have to concentrate your attention on those you wish to know. This perfume is quite effective for those who wish to meet people for casual relationships.

LOVE INCENSE An incense made from Rue, Musk, Ambergris and Benzoin. A bit of iron powder or ocher is added to the finished product, which is then ground again in the mortar.   When this incense is burned while you perform a suitable love ritual the force of the ritual is greatly amplified.

LOVE ME (Quiereme) PERFUME   Used to attract a marriage partner, this perfume contains a bit of orange extract. Household orange extract added to the favorite perfume is often used, but a better perfume is the following.

Orange extract, orange zest, Damania, a bit of brown sugar and crushed Juniper berries. Use in a cottonseed oil base, for a high relationship, or in a peanut oil base for a low, primarily sexual, relationship. For catching a specific marital partner, add vervain and pray over the oil, asking for the partner using both names.

Another good oil to use to meet a marriage partner is Sweet Pea two parts and Geranium oil ½ part, in a perfume diluent base.

LOVE POWDER   The best love powder for an established relationship is to put a bit of Ginger and a bit of Cardamom seed powders between the sheets of the marital bed. This adds a more exciting vibration to the bedroom, which may assist in spicing up a long lasting relationship. Too much of this powder, or too frequent use, may make sleep difficult.

LOVE AND SUCCESS OIL   Assists in happiness in marriage and in life. This oil is used for anointing red and pink candles when praying for love, marriage, or success in the relationship. It is made from Red Poppy and sandalwood in an Almond oil base.

LOVE POWDER   For some reason, there are people who demand love powder of a specific color. While the obvious colors for these powders should be pink and red, but blue, yellow, purple, and even black are often requested. This may be accomplished by coloring Orrisroot, or even talcum powder, to suit an individuals taste. Using colored powders, the so-called love powder may be made up in any color designed.

LOVER'S POWDER   Lover's powder is a powder made up in, conjure bag, or obeah bag, or charm bag, all of these the

136

same item with another name. There are any number of variations of this powder, but most of the ones that work contain cinnamon, Myrrh, Sandalwood, and something to dissipate the vibration out into the universe, a lodestone, camphor, or some alcohol. They have even been made up with mothballs, which I do not recommend. This is not a magic powder spell, but rather a spell to force love.

LOVER'S INCENSE (Amantes) Used to increase a person's natural sexual magnetism. It makes the person seem more magnetic and sensual. Copal incense base with ground amber, used in a full body fumigation.

Opoponox Oil in winters bark, used in a fumigation in the bedroom while dressing, will work wonders if it is used before going out on a date.

LOW JOHN [Trillium Pendulum] [#2337] Same as Bethroot, Which see. Used to remove curses by chewing some of the root and spiting it out on the ground.

It is also known as Low John the Conqueror, as well as Trillium, or Cough Root. It is protective of other work being done, and is added to charm bags for that purpose. Also placed in a room, usually over the doorway, to make negative influences uncomfortable in the room. It is occasionally placed under a bed or sewn into a pillow for the same purpose. The carved root is used in pendulum divination, as the bob of the pendulum.

LUCK AROUND BUSINESS POWDER A powder used by self-employed merchants to increase their business. It draws new customers, and is said to work well at increasing the business and trade of stores and salesmen.

> Cinquefoil powder - ½ ounce
> Cinnamon powder - ½ ounce
> Orris root Powder - 1 ounce

The powders should be sifted together several times to mix them well, and set aside to blend for a week or two. In use, it is spread around a business place. Prostitutes often put a pinch in their pubic hair; salesmen rub their hands with a pinch of the powder.

LUCKY SHOE POWDER   This powder is made from equal parts of basil leaves, cinnamon powder and iron filings. It is rubbed inside shoes, and is prayed over to keep the person on their proper path in life.

Used to bless a new pair of shoes, it can bless old shoes as well. Use only a small amount of powder for each shoe, just rub into the shoes with the intent of blessing them.

LUCKY HAND - Mojo Hand   This is a charm bag that has been prepared by a Practitioner. There are a wide variety of them in use, and an infinite number of them that may be made.

One which is filled with a variety of herbs, usually includes Devils Shoestring, Cinquefoil, and John the Conqueror root. A silver coin is often included. It is then prayed over and fed with whiskey or rum. The person using it must feed their Lucky Hand with a few drops of rum or whiskey every week. It is to be carried on their person at all times. The owner is to rub their hands with it when calling on its luck bestowing power.

LUCKY LODESTONE   (Suerte de Piedra Iman)   This is another charm made for the client by a practitioner. When it is made, the client is given specific instructions concerning its use and care. Lodestones are always fed with iron filings, often with a liquor, either whiskey or rum, and sometimes with coins.

As these lodestones are always made for specific purposes in the individuals life, they often have wide variations in the details of their care and treatment.

LUCKY MYSTIC POWDER   Used to attract good to the user, usually thorough dreams. Mullein leaf powder and Benzoin will accomplish this if the two are aged together for a week or more. Dilute by a third with Talc.

LUCKY SEVEN ROOT   Protection against being hexed or crossed by an unknown enemy. This root is said to be especially good when used while gambling or taking any other kind of risk. It is made of a whole Queen Elisabeth root. If it is being prepared for someone it should be ritually prayed over.

138

L

LUCKY SPIRIT POWDER   A Hex breaking powder, made of ground garlic powder. To be put in the corners of the home.

LUNGWORT   Leaves   (Pulmonaria Officinalis)   [#1854] Said to be an excellent cough remedy.

13

M

MACE (Myristica Fragrans) [#1542] The outer covering of the nutmeg. A male herb of Jupiter, used both in magic, and as a spice ingredient. Magically, it is used in controlling incenses in matters of love and honor. It has a martial vibration that may be used for many things. Good in incense, useless in a bath, fair as an additive in a powder.

MAGNET POWDER Magnet powder consists of pulverized iron filings that are used in charms, added to other magic powders, and used by themselves. Alone, magnet powders are used to feed lodestones in one of the many spells that use lodestones, such as marriage spells, money spells, and similar prosperity spells.

Magnet powder is a primary constituent of Magnetic Water and Magnetic Earth, and is used as an attraction force in a variety of ways in a large number of other spells. Iron filings are a symbol of Mars, and may be used as in spells to energize male sexual energy, as wall as being usable in any spell where the masculine inquiring-conceptive principle is required to have an active role.

M

Because of their variety of uses, iron filings have a number of names; Lodestone powder, Magnetic sand, Magnetic powder, Magnet dust, and Iron powder are the most common.

The best place to purchase fine iron filings is from stores that sell educational material to schools and teachers. Machine shops are also a good source, as are scientific supply houses. If you purchase these filings by the pound, you will be doing well.

MAGNETIC SAND   Iron Filings, which see, and see above as well.

MAGNOLIA BARK (Magnolia Glauca) [#1425] It makes a good tonic, and is also good for reducing fever and cold symptoms.   The Magnolia flower is sometimes used in love charms.

MAGIC CARPET OIL   An oil used for Astral projection, usually a hallucinatory surfactant.   The standard witches 'flying ointment' of the middle ages contained poison hemlock, deadly nightshade, poplar leaves, wolf's bane, and soot. This is hardly anything to play with, and it is not ever recommended for use.

MAGUEY   Sacred to the Yoruba Mother Goddess Yemaya It is used primarily for negative work. 'When Maguey falls into the river the turtles and fishes that live there must die.'

MAIDENHAIR (Adiantum Pedatum) [#69] (A Capillus Veneris)   An excellent aid in the relief of coughs and congestion. Ruled by Venus, it is used in love spells. Used to bring beauty and love into the life, it is used in charm bags for this purpose.

MALE FERN ROOT (Aspidium Filix Mas) [#303] Buckhorn Brake   The root is used in expelling tapeworms, and in magic for love spells. Is this a comment on the nature of love?

MALVA FLOWERS   Black   (Malva Sylvestris)   [#1434]
The plant and flowers are used in healing. The flower petals
are used in incense.

MANACA ROOT   (Brunfelsia Hopeana ?)   [?]   It is said to
be one of the best remedies for rheumatism and arthritis.
However, it is a doubtful remedy.

MANGO   Mangifera Indica   [#1435]   The leaves are used
to purify the blood. A bath of the stewed and macerated leaves
is used to assist a pregnant woman in childbirth. The entire
fruit is edible and may be cooked for medicinal use.

MANDRAKE   Root   (Atropa Mandragora)   [#328]   Much
heard about, little seen, most of the mandrake sold by occult
shops is a false product. The root may be made to grow into
any shape desired, which is why it is so popular in image magic.
However, the same thing may be accomplished with many other
roots. Mandrake has as many magical legends surrounding its
use as the difficulty of obtaining any real mandrake root would
permit.
Medically, the root was once used for hallucinations,
delirium, or death. It is a narcotic poison, once used as a pain
reliever or anesthetic.

MANDRAKE   Oil, or Perfume   Seldom made and seldom
used. To be valid it must have a piece of true mandrake root in
the bottle.   Otherwise it is usually just colored mineral oil.
Peanut oil would be a better choice, as it is a better match for
the mandrake root.   The oil may be used for either blessing,
hexing or protecting. The oil works well with the elements, but
not as well as sandalwood or cedar oils.

MANDRAKE   (Podophyllum   Peltatum)   [#1764]
(American or False Mandrake) May Apple   Medically, it is a
good physic. The root is used in image magic, and in ritual
magic incenses.

MANO PONDEROSO   Five Finger Grass, or cinquefoil,
which see.

142

M

MAN TRAP (Trampa de Hombre)   Perfume Sweet pea and violet in a perfume oil base, with a bit of red sandalwood powder in the bottle.

MANY THOUGHTS   A powder used to break a person's concentration. It is used to make a person think so many things at the same time they cannot focus on anything. It makes them incompetent for a time.

The powder is also known as Monkey Mind, Million Thoughts, and Worry Powder. It is prayed over by name, and either cast or blown on the person to be harmed.

Powdered White Chestnut Leaves - 1 ounce
In some cases, Black Poplar leaves are also added

If the powder is to be diluted, something that is not advised, the diluted it should be diluted with Orrisroot powder on an equal weight basis. Diluting this powder with inorganic material will ground out its action.

MAPLE (Acer Dasycarpum) [#28]   A decoction of the leaves and bark is said to strengthen the liver. Taking a bath in a tea made of the seeds is said to assist in astral projection. I seriously doubt both of these assertions.

MARIE LAVEAU PEACE WATER   A very diluted perfumed water, containing about a drop of floral perfume to a quart of water. It is used as a home sprinkle for placing a good vibration in the home. What is actually placed in the home depends on the charge given by the prayer of the spiritual practitioner. This water is usually prepared and charged by the practitioner following a consultation. The name, and the often very fancy label on the bottle made it easier for the client to accept this water, and sprinkle it in their home.

MARIGOLD   Flor de Muerto   [Calendula Officinalis] [#460]   Ruled by the Sun.   Used in love sachets, to attract love, add Marigold tea to the bath water for attaining love, and for drawing good things to you.   Used for burns, insect bites and poisons. Several cups of the tea each day, up to ten, are suggested for those who have an ulcerous cancer.

The tea in a bath, or on a compress, strengthens the astral fabric. Used in the pillow or bed it makes the dreams more real, bringing the astral plane closer to the dreamer. A simple but excellent fluid condenser, a tea made from the flowers is a strong astral fortifier. It is used to make magic mirrors, and in a poultice for strengthening the individual in injury or illnesses. A few drops of the alcoholic tincture on a charm bag will keep the charm on 'target.'

The tincture is of great assistance in connecting the astral and physical planes. While the tea is a curative for some kinds of cancer, it will also be found useful for healing other conditions, used as either a poultice or a plaster. It is often used in a salve for its healing effects.

The herb is an excellent astral condenser, used magically in many ways, either as a tea or incense. The succus (a strong alcoholic tincture) is specifically used for coating magic mirrors.

MARJORAM Leaves Amraco [Origanum Marjorana] [#1618] Majorana Hortensis Moench Ruled by Venus The dried herb and leaves of a bushy perennial of the mint family. Used as a sweeping herb to remove negativity, it is not very strong in this respect, but it does have some effect. The herb is carried as a charm against witchcraft. Place some of the powdered herb in each corner of the rooms of a dwelling, and renew it each month. Best for producing positive changes in the home, it is not much good for most other matters. (Doing this is supposed to draw a husband, which seems not to happen.)

It may be added to food as a love potion after praying over it for the effect desired. Also used as a sweeping herb, to remove negativity from a room or any place where it is used as a sweeping compound.

Medically, it is used as an aid in cases of upset stomach.

MARAVILLA Marvel of Peru, which see.

MARVEL OF PERU Marvilla Marabilis Jalapa [#1501] The root is a cathartic, and is used in magic in the same

M

manner as Jalap Root.   An alcoholic version is commercially available.

MASTER MICHAEL SCOTT'S PILLS   He was the Physician Royal and Astrologer to Frederic II, the Holy Roman Emperor. These pills were first prepared by him about 1220 AD.   They have had a good reputation ever since, being supposedly for the preservation of youth and the prevention of the physical decadence that precede old age.   3 Oz. by weight of Hepatic Aloes   1 Oz. By weight of each of these: Bryony: Indian, Belleric and Emblic Myrobalans; Lemons; Mastic; Scammony; Hazel; Roses; Rhubarb.

They are to be mixed together in the juice of cabbages, and formed into pills of medium size. The dosage is to take four or five of these pills every day.

So much for medieval medicine.

MASTERWORT   (Heracleum Lanatum)   [#1148]   It is said to be good in the treatment of colds, flu, cramps, spasms, headaches, and nervous tension. The root and seed are used. The leaves of the herb in oil are used for treating neck pains with a physical cause.

Ruled by Mars, it is a herb of power, courage, and protection. It is used for this purpose in charm bags. The powder of the root is also used as a controlling incense in rituals.

MASTIC GUM   From the mastich Tree [Pistacio Lentiscus] [#1741]   Used as a purifying incense in Voodoo rituals. The gum is also used to fill cavities in the teeth.

Mastic may be burned alone, or with other incenses. It is one of the basic ingredients of many types of incense, especially as filler in some so called church incenses.

MATE   Yerba Green   Rompe Zaraguey   [Ilex Paraguaiensis]   [#1206]   The tea removes astral negativity of all kinds from people, places or things. Very good when used as a bath or as a floor wash.

Used to remove influences of spirits of the dead, it is also used as a blow powder, being blown on the body of the person to be protected. See Yerba Mate.

MAYWEED (Anthemis Catula) [#1440] A good general tonic, and anti spasmodic. A nervine used for the relief of headache.

MEADOWSWEET (Spiraea Ulmaria) [#2214] Useful in the treatment of diarrhea. Used as an incense, it was sacred to the druids. Often strewn through the house to add a freshness to it.

MEDITATION (Meditacion) Oil This oil is used by those who meditate, to assist them in quieting the mind and calming themselves. The oil is made from Olive oil with Louts and Orrisroot powder. Iris (Orris) perfume oil may be added if desired.

MERCURY (Mecurio) OIL Supposedly to be applied to the forehead while doing readings. This oil is supposedly to be used to gain access to seeing into the future. The occult store version is often plain colored mineral oil with a drop of toxic elemental Mercury added to the bottle.
A better blend would be Walnut Oil with a little powdered Cinnamon, Celery seed, Mace, Clove, and Storax, in it.

MERCURY Metallic mercury, which is a very toxic heavy metal, and the oxides of Mercury, are often added to spells as expediters. Their purpose is to make spells work faster. All of these compounds of mercury are poisonous. While Red Mercuric Oxide (Polvo Rojo or red powder) has been proven the best expediter for most work, none of them are recommended for use. These substances directly attack the brain, causing a reduction of the mental function.

MESCAL BUTTONS (Lopophora Lewinii) [NONE] Peyote A tonic is made from this fungus for use in Angina Pectoris and other cardiac conditions. It is a dangerous hallucinogenic and narcotic.

M

MILK THISTLE (Cnicus Lanceolata) [#672] The herb and extract are used to heal liver problems. Available as a standardized product for this purpose. (From Thysilyn in Germany.)

Also see: Silybum Marianum [#502] Carduus Marianus The Mary Thistle. A bitter tonic. Seeds and Herb are used.

MIMOSA MAGIC OIL Made from the powdered dried flowers of Mimosa, it is diluted with Sunflower seed oil and made into a body oil. It is to be applied to the whole body before going to sleep, to produce true dreams. It may be used to anoint blue and white candles that are burned together, with a prayer for either a true dream or a favorable change in the condition of life. A few drops may also be used in a bath. This oil is used successfully in "sleeping in the temple" as a way to change the conditions of the person's life.

MINT See Spearmint and Peppermint They are Herbs of Leo and Venus, sacred to various deities, according to the culture. Used as mental stimulants in teas, they are used for protection in most spells, probably because of the sharp smell and taste. They are used in love spells to affect the beloved's mind.

MISTLETOE (Muerdago) (Viscum Flavescens) [#2437] {Viscum Album} Called Heal All It is a parasite plant, living on other plants, and thus becomes the symbol of spirit, living on the body. It was a sacred herb to the ancient Druids of England, and thus much used by those who consider themselves Druids today.

Mistletoe is also a symbol of resurrection, and rebirth, as well as a symbol of death. The crushed berries as well as the leaves are used in magic. It is used as an incense, and as a sprinkle or wash. Used in love spells. Medically, it has been used as a nervine. The Perfume has a Gardenia scent, although it should have three to seven of the mistletoe berries in the bottle. The leaves do not make a very good incense, although the effect is there, the scent is lacking. Smell's like burning vegetables.

MOJO   This is an African word meaning Spell. Like Ju Ju, which applies to the entire range of African magical practices, MoJo can apply to any one of an infinite number of magical spells.   Thus there are 'Mojo Bags,' and 'Mojo Charms' and some people say that their 'Mojo' is what protects them.

It has nothing to do with one's sexuality.

MONEY   (Dinero) OIL   A Green oil used to anoint the green candles used in money spells. The oil is often used as an incense in these spells by placing a few drops of the oil on hot charcoal as the candles are lit and the prayer made. A drop or two may also be used as a polish to clean and polish the cash register drawers in a business, for drawing more money to them.

Money oil is best made from cypress oil, honeysuckle, peppermint, and mineral oil. It should have about one or two drops of cedar wood oil for each eight ounces of Money Oil, to stabilize the elemental forces being worked with. This is a popular and highly successful oil.

MONEY DRAWING OIL   (Niebla de Dinero)   The best money drawing oil is made as in the formula above. Adding magnetic sand (Iron Filings) or Ocher (Iron Oxide) to the blended, aged and filtered oil product enhances its money drawing qualities.   A lodestone or magnet is added to the bottle, and it is prayed over to draw money to the person it has been made for.

MONEY MIST   (Niebla de Dinero)   A sprinkle or spray of money drawing water. Made of the money oil given above, tap water and a bit of dish soap. Spray from a spray bottle to put the money vibe in the room.

MONEY POWDER   Made from Cinnamon and Nutmeg diluted with talc. Benzoin may be added if desired.

MONEY DRAWING POWDER   This powder is effective in bringing money to the person using it, as well as protecting them form financial loss. It may also be used to give assistance in obtaining employment. To use, put a pinch on the sternum while praying for money. Rub the remaining dust on your hands by wringing them together. The cooking spices work better than most of the more exotic mixes.

> Cinnamon – ½ ounce
> Nutmeg – 1 ounce
> Clove - ¼ Ounce

Mix and sift several times, then store in an amber bottle for a week before using.

MOTHERWORT [Leonurus Cardiaca] [#1326] Lion's Ear   A tea of the leaves is used in a bath for a more loving nature. Its presence in the front yard is said to protect all of the family from harm. Used for female disorders and to strengthen the heart. Ruled by Venus.

MUGWORT [Artemisia Vulgaris] [#273] Ruled by Venus   Burned as an incense while crystal gazing, to increase psychic vision. It can cause prophetic dreams by placing the leaf powder in a red charm bag, which is kept under the pillow at night. Burned as an incense in the bedroom to promote dreaming. It is used in making the so-called dream pillows. It is burned with incense in spiritualist work, to encourage the spirits to speak.

Carried in a red charm bag to keep from tiring while traveling, it was first brought to the North America by the Pilgrims for this purpose. Once used instead of hops in beer making. It is used in Chinese Moxibustion, a treatment used in acupuncture. Medically, it is a good remedy for all female problems relating to the menstrual cycle.

MULLEIN [Verbascum Thapsus] [#2401] Ruled by Saturn. The leaves are used as an incense in black magic rituals. It should be kept near the entryway to a house to bar witchcraft from entering the home. A fluid condenser for crystals. Used for casting spells on others. Mullein seeds from the candle take a nice magical charge and may be used as a casting powder alone. It can be added to love spells as a domination powder. Medically, it is used for lung disorders. A cough syrup is made from the plant. Also excellent in cases of suppressed menstruation and cramps.

MURIA PUAMA (Liriosma Ovata) [NONE] A Brazilian herb, used for male sexual rejuvenation. A nerve stimulant, and supposedly an aphrodisiac and potency restorer for men. The root is steeped in brandy for at least two weeks. The dose is a wine glass, (Two Ounces) of the brandy every night.

MUSK CRYSTALS These are the crystallized extract of the odoriferous glands from the testicles of the Musk Ox of the Northern Tibetan Plains. Only the synthetic is available today at anything like a reasonable price.

MUSK LOVE POWDER Usually made by adding Hoyt's musk oil to talcum powder. Allow to sit for a week or more. Apply to the body after a bath, but use sparingly, as the scent is strong.

MUSTARD SEED Mostaza (Yellow, Black or Red) (Sinapis Alba, Negra) [#2154] The seed of a number of hardy adaptable annual herbs that thrive in temperate climates, the mustard seed is a symbol of faith in the Christian religion. (Matthew 13:31 - 32) Included in spells and charm bags as a token of faith. Supposedly protective, it is said to revive the spirits. May be used in negative magic as well.

(Sinapis alba L. WHITE or YELLOW MUSTARD) The BLACK MUSTARD SEED (Brassica Nigra (L.) Koch.) and the BROWN MUSTARD SEED (Brassica Juncea Coss & Czern) are used in magic to increase strife and dissent among people. Not a very good incense, it repulses cold and chill in the room. It is better used in charms, where it is effective in love spells. The mustard plaster is used in healing chest complaints by adding heat to the surface of the skin.

To make a tree barren, take dried rose buds and mustard seeds and grind them to a fine powder. Sprinkle the mixture around the trunk of the tree on the first evening of the full moon, and the tree will bear no fruit.

M

Often chewed for toothache, or used as a poultice or plaster for pain, to cure congested lungs, or to draw splinters. An old time remedy, still of some use.

BLACK MUSTARD SEED (Sinapis Nigra) [#2157] Cast on the doorsteps of an enemy to cause strife in their life. Cast on the floor of a room to cause dissension in the room.

MYRRH Gum (Commiphora Molmol) [#?] An incense gum resin of plant origin (The Myrrh tree) that brings the astral realms closer to the physical realm. It is the oldest of the gum resin incenses.

Myrrh is burned in a mixture with Frankincense, making up the most common "Church Incense." Myrrh is also used as an incense in love rituals, or in any other work where it is desired to lower the astral realms to the physical. This is not always a good thing for everyone to do, but many people use it for this purpose. This is why Myrrh is the incense of choice in summoning to visible appearance. It is widely used in magical and occult ritual work for this purpose.

An antiseptic, it is often used as a mouthwash, and to assist in healing minor sores or abscesses in the mouth. Myrrh has been used in medicine for its antiseptic qualities over the years. Myrrh and Golden Seal are the most common blend for a healing herbal mouthwash.

MYRRH POWDER   Myrrh is an agent of manifestation, making it easier for the forms of the astral realm to become visible, and act in the physical world. Its use as a magic powder comes as no surprise. As a casting powder, it is used around altars, and on the floor of rooms in which séances and rituals are held. As incense, it is used in summoning to visual appearance. The user should always have a clear intent as what it is desired that Myrrh powder should do for them.

MYRTLE LEAVES   [Myrtus Conmunis]   [#1550] {Vaccinium Frondosum}   Ruled by Venus. The primary home blessing incense. Used for inspiration as an incense. Used to preserve youth and love. Myrtle tea was once prescribed to be taken every three days for this purpose. "Angle Water," made of cold steeped myrtle tea, orange water, and rose water, was once quite popular as a refreshing drink.

Inhaling the vapors of an infusion of Myrtle relieves the head pains caused by a severe cold. It can also be used as a soothing compress on the head, and used as a poultice for cuts, bruises, and scratches.

Myrtle leaves are an ingredient of one of the most popular House Blessing Incenses. When placed in the path of a loved one, it is supposed to guide their feet to your door. Myrtle is also known as bayberry, which see. It is also a popular magical "Blow Powder" which is used to rapidly change conditions in a person's life, depending the prayer made over it. Myrtle is often used in love incenses to draw the beloved.

14

N

NETTLE HERB   Leaves and Root   [Urtica Dioica] [#2363]   A mild diuretic. Used as a curse breaker, but there are many others that are more effective. It may be used in binding rituals. The stinging hairs of the seed bulb are used in potions as an aphrodisiac. Ruled by Mars in Aries, it is a martial herb.

It may be used to separate two people without pain to them if you weave a mat of the herb, and place it under their doormat. Sprinkle the powdered herb around your home, to remove any curses that may have been placed on you, or on your house.

It arrests bleeding, and is a good gargle for sore throat. Also good for healing burns. An excellent blood purifier. It can curdle milk without leaving a bad taste, which is useful in cheese and yogurt making. It is a blistering agent as well.

NEVER FORGET ME AND LOVE ME FOREVER (Quiereme Siempre)   A perfume that is used to make someone think about another, keeping thoughts of them in their mind. If you carefully wipe up the gum trace left by a snail as it walks over a clean windowpane, you will have a gum that can accomplish this. Place the snail gum on a photograph of the person, and pray over it for this effect. You can also place the snail on the photograph and have the snail travel all over it. The prayer over the snail-slimed photograph is what accomplished the task.

NIGHT BLOOMING CEREUS   (Cereus (or Cactus) Grandiflorus) [#437]   A cardiac stimulant, tonic and diuretic, as well as used for relieving nervous and menstrual headaches. The flowers and stems are a sedative.

NIGHTSHADE, DEADLY   (Atropa Belladonna)   (See Belladonna) [#327]   A narcotic, sedative, and anti spasmodic. Valuable in the treatment of the eyes, as it dilates the pupil. Relieves pain, and aids circulation. Once given in small doses to protect from scarlet fever. A Poison, not suggested for use.

NINE MYSTERY OIL (Nueve Mistyerio)   Used for blessing people and overcoming difficulties. It may be added to water to make a room sprinkle, or used as a floor wash. Used to anoint candles for success or for a change of fortune. This oil is made of nine oils, Almond, Canola, Cotton Seed, Mineral, Olive, Peanut, Safflower, Sunflower, and Walnut in equal quantities. It is to be consecrated in the name of the nine mysteries of the Sacraments of the Roman Catholic Church.

NIRVANA INCENSE   Used to heighten psychic powers. Often found to be useful in spirit communications, and in some meditation sessions. Made of equal quantities of Benzoin and Copal gums, either used as mixed, or diluted with equal quantities of Winters bark.

NO HEX POWDER   An Unhexing powder used as a blow powder and as a remedy for minor headaches and pains. It is not a medicinal powder. It may be put into the hair at the new Moon with a prayer that it keeps hexes away. This should be done ritually, as a candle burning ceremony, with an uncrossing incense burning when the prayer for protection is made. The powder is made from cornstarch, rice flour powder, and magnetic sand (Iron Filings).   The No Hex ritual includes blowing a pinch of the powder to the four corners of the room, as well as placing a pinch of the powder in the hair. The ritual may be performed every month with good results.

A Jamaican Obeah man, who used to live in my neighborhood, had a regular ritual service using this powder with his clients every month. The ritual involved prayers for his clients for a good month, and prayers for their protection. He then applied this powder to their heads. The service was always well attended.

NUTGALL   [Quercus Infectoria]   [#1888]   Also known as the Mad Apple. It is the fruit of the Gall Oak. It may be added to incense in jinxing and hexing rituals, where it will turn a person, or their life, sour.

NUTMEG   Nuez Moscada   (Myristica Moschata)   [#1542] (Myristica Fragrans Houtt.)   Used primarily in money charms. As an incense it radiates heat energy into the room. One of the most powerful lucky talismans of the Voodoo or Hoodoo worker is the prepared gamblers nutmeg. The nut is also carried for prosperity, and for general good luck. It must be kept in charm bag and carried whenever you are gambling. Jupiter rules the nutmeg.

Powdered nutmeg, when used in a tea, for a bath makes people more open to listening to you. The nutmeg bath is good to take before a job interview. Use a cup of tea in your bath. Nutmeg incense is good for opening communications in a room or area. Burn a quarter teaspoon of powdered nutmeg on charcoal.

Medically, it is an aromatic and a stimulant. An aid to digestion if a few drops of the oil are taken on a lump of sugar. It is used to induce sleep by rubbing the oil on the temples. It has a mild hallucinogenic effect if taken in quantity. (1 or 2 teaspoons) However, it is often toxic to people in that dose.

NUX VOMICA   (Strychnos Nux Vomica)   [#2235]   The seeds are used. It acts on the cerebro-spinal system, and is a sleep inducing nervine when properly used. However, it is a deadly poison, and must be used with great care.   In homeopathic dilution, it is known as the corpse reviver, and is useful for many of the illnesses of modern life.

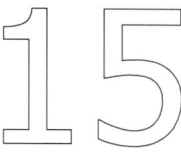

O

OBEAH   Originally an African term referring generally to the cosmic power. Thus Baraka, or Universal Life Force. It is generally a Jamaican term, which has developed a range of meanings. It now refers to the folk magic practiced in Jamaica, and among African Americans and those in the Caribbean generally. It is equivalent to Hoodoo and Root work, in that it refers to folk magic, not to any specific religion.

A Wanga, or Oanga, is a spell cast or a charm made by Obeah, just as a Mojo is a spell cast or a charm made by Hoodoo. These products have natural inherent power by virtue of their ingredients, and the combinations of the ingredients used to produce the charm. Thus they require no consecration or prayer, as is more common in European derived magical practice. However, prayer is often done to increase the effect of the charm.

OBEAH PERFUME OIL   (So Called)   An Oil used to anoint candles and people, add to the bath, and bless rooms or ritual fixtures. Also known as dressing oil, this is the most general-purpose oil there is, as it is useful for all positive ends. Contains about an ounce of finely powdered Frankincense, and about an eighth of a teaspoon of finely powdered sea salt in eight ounces of olive oil. Refrigerate after making the oil, and shake well before using. The scent used with this oil is usually a spicy scent. This oil does not come from the Obeah practice of Jamaica. It originated in New York City in the 1940's.

OBITSU POWDER The powder left behind when termites have eaten a fallen Red Camwood tree. Apprentices in divination gather it at the new moon, it is carefully sifted free of all foreign matter and dried thoroughly and given to their teacher, who either pronounces it good or discards it. If it is found to be good, it is placed in leather bags and stored for use in divination.

It is a deep red powder, and looks like fine Georgia red clay, but it is only available in Africa, and usually used only by those who are initiates in the divination practice. Don't believe you can buy it here, as it is unavailable.

ORANGE OIL Available in a number of varieties. 'Portugal oil' is the sweet oil of the orange peel, as opposed to 'Biçarade,' which is bitter orange peel oil. Neroli is the orange flower essential oil, the product used in most magic spells that uses orange oil. Petitgrain is the oil of the leaves of the Orange tree.

Orange oil is used to bring a relationship to the altar. Anointing three candles with the oil and burning them in a marital spell will usually convince the reluctant suitor to propose marriage.

ORRIS ROOT POWDER IRIS POWDER Finely powdered Orris root is used as a condiment in Europe. It is also used in cleansing and love spells, but its greatest effect is to improve communications between people, as well as between the physical and non-physical worlds. This powder takes a charge very well, so it may be used in blessing, and in prayer.

The root is carried as a love charm.

Orris Oil, Perfume, and Incense, may also be used to promote communication with the astral realms.

O

I have found one of the best blessing powders is a mixture of ground Orrisroot and ground Lotus root powders. This powder in Olive oil makes an excellent blessing oil.

P

PAINT   Powders and chalks of various kinds may be added to paint to influence the 'feeling' or 'vibration' of a room. Usually a teaspoon of the finely ground powder or chalk is added to each gallon of the paint used to coat the room or area to be influenced. A friend suggested adding various powders to the drywall compound used in new construction and remodeling for this purpose.

PAPYRUS   A paper made of the Papyrus reeds grown in the Egyptian Nile. A much better papyrus paper is infrequently available commercially today.   It is considerably better for wrting spells and charms, and for other magical work, than the parchment paper these sigils, charms, and so forth are usually drawn on.

PASSION FLOWER   (Flor de Pasion)   Despite its name, this herb is a strong sedative.   The Oil and Perfume are artificial.

PATCHOULI   (Patchuli)   The Herb, Oil and Perfume are known for going both ways.   Useful in either positive or negative magic, this favorite scent of the nineteen sixties should

160

P

always be worn or used with care, as it can be charged and used against the wearer. It may be used both for love spells and for separations. It is a useful material, but is often difficult to work with.

PEACE POWDER   A powder to be sprinkled on the heads of quarreling parties to put an end to their mutual strife. It has its origin in African crown courts, and as there is no specific powder suiting all occasions, a generic substitute may be made. You can take your choice.

PEONY   (Peonia)   Peony seeds are the 'Jumby Beans' used to cause problems with people. Casting either whole or ground jumby beans around a room will cause dissension and trouble among the people in the room.

PEPPERMINT   (Menta)   A mental stimulant, the leaves and oil are used in any number of spells for this purpose.

PEARL MOSS   Used in protection spells. I find it not to be as effective as other spell ingredients.

PINE   (Pino)   If you have been using pine scented products in you home and are having problems, switch cleansers. Pine scent is not beneficial for everyone. In some instances, non-physical difficulties in the home may be traced to the use of pine scented cleansing products.

POWDER OF THE DEAD   This powder is made by necromancers and some initiates of religious practices that work with the dead, from the scrapings of the skull (bone) of the deceased. Other material is added to this powder suitable to the work at hand. It is a formidable powder used for working magic of various kinds. The spirit of the deceased is added to the powder by vivification with alcohol. Alchemical alcohol is preferably, but not usually, used for this purpose.
Another powder of the dead is made from scrapings of various other bones, thighbones, leg bones and foot bones (For mobility), Arm, finger, and hand bones (For dexterity), along with the skull (For guidance). This powder may be made into a

very protective powder, which may be used to keep spirits away from a place or a location. It may also be added to paint to protect a room, or even an entire building.

Another 'powder of the dead' is made from the disintegrating remains of a body, to which scrapings of bones are often added.

One of the African 'Preservers Of Communal Morality' religious cults made a powder from the disintegrating remains of bodies of those who have died of smallpox. It was used to cause those whom the cult wished to kill to become infected with the disease.

PROTECTION POWDER   Should another blend of protection powder be desired, it might be advisable to find out what one wishes to be protected against and look for a powder that will work toward that end.

General Purpose Protection Powder

Ground Cloves   1 Ounce
Powered Frankincense   ½ Ounce
Powdered Camphor   ¼ Ounce
Powdered Cinnamon   ¼ Ounce

Sift together well, place in an amber bottle, and let it digest in a warm place for a week, shaking occasionally. After digesting, add the above mixture to seven ounces of talcum powder and sift together several times to obtain a complete mixture. To use, apply on the sternum after bathing in the morning.

Protects against the bad vibes of others and most negative influences that may be sent against you. It has a beneficial effect on most people, but if a rash develops, discontinue using it.

For Protection Against Curses Sent By Religious Christians

Ground Verbena Herb   ¼ Ounce
Powdered Galangal   ¼ Ounce
Powdered Rue Herb   ¼ Ounce
Powdered Cinnamon   ¼ Ounce

Sift together several times to mix well. Use on the head, hands and feet, and rub on the body as well. This is used to

P

avoid curses placed by those who claim to be Christians. To protect against curses by Jewish religious persons substitute Hyssop for Rue in the above formula.

The 81st Psalm may be prayed over the powder to charge it for protection in either case.

Q

Q PERFUME OIL   Stimulating perfume oil used for enticement and seduction by women. A bit of Capsicum and Moss Rose added to any regular perfume oil will accomplice this quite nicely.

QUINCE SEED   Supposedly protective, I have not found this to be particularly effective.

QUITTING POWDER   A powder used to make someone "quit." It is the same as STOP powder. It may be used in any number of cases when the desire is to force a stopping of something, or of someone.   It may be made up and kept on hand indefinitely in the uncharged state.

Pumice stone, from Volcanic Lava   1 ounce
Reduce to a fine powder in the mortar and set aside.
Coal ½ Ounce
Reduce to a fine powder in the mortar and set aside.
Mix the two powders in the mortar sifting them well together. This mixed powder may be stored indefinitely.

To use, take the amount of the mixture desired and activate by placing in the hand with a drop or two of whiskey rum or

Q

vodka. Pray over the powder, calling by name the person who is to be stopped, and in what way they are to be stopped. The paste of the powder and alcohol should be allowed to dry back to the powder state and the powder may be sprinkled on the person's path. It may also be used as a blow powder, or it may be rubbed on the person. It will very effectively stop a person who is attempting to influence someone in any way.

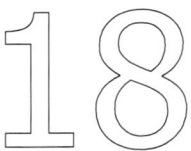

R

RECONCILIATION POWDER   Myrtle and Gardenia perfume and flower powder added to talc will promote a reconciliation with a former lover. You must bear in mind that reconciliation always changes the relationship, and not always for the better.

REPENTANT POWDER   A powder used in encouraging someone to be repentant, usually repentant of a specific act, sometimes becoming repentant of their sins in general. This powder is a worry powder, in that it brings out feelings of guilt and sin from the persons sub conscious mind. Emotions of sin and guilt are not a part of a well-developed persons life, as they act to block the

R

life. Obviously, bringing these emotions out in a person is of dubious value to them at best.

Powdered Rue Herb   ½ Ounce
Powdered Hyssop Herb   ½ Ounce
Consecrated Salt   ¼ Ounce
Orrisroot Powder ¼ Ounce

Sift together, mixing well. Store in a closed container in a dark place. Use as a blow powder after charging by name, and mentioning the specific deed or act you desire them to repent.

REMOVING SPELLS   To remove someone from your life use the four thieves' vinegar spell, which see. To remove them from your neighborhood use deer horn shavings aas a casting powder in their path. To get rid of someone at a bar, put some of your nail filings in their drink.

ROMPE ZARAGUAY POWDER   A blow powder used to remove negative influences in the Caribbean version of the Yoruba African magical religious practice. In theory it is made from leaves of a plant specially gathered by initiates, and prepared by those who are initiates in the practice.

That's the romantic view.

A good substitute for this powder is Mate herb, as is used to make Mate Tea. The powdered herb works as well as the prepared herb, and is more easily available. This is not a good uncrossing powder in any event, see Flying Devil Powder.

ROOT WORK   A form of African American magical practice, in which roots are used in performing magic. Chosen for their magical virtue, the roots are used to make charms of different kinds for various purposes. This is a primarily Christian magical practice, but religion is not actually a part of the practice. It is often blended with African American Hoodoo magical practice.

ROSE   (Rosa)   Incense, Oil, Powder, etc.   All of these are usually made from artificial red rose oil, as pure Rose Otto, the natural essential oil of rose, is quite expensive. The stick rose incense is the best general-purpose incense that may be used, it has a nice calming effect, and as it only works on the positive side, it is discouraging to negative work. Rose is one of the most popular incense and perfume scents known to man.

ROSEMARY   (Romero)   Kitchen rosemary may be used to put a pleasant vibration in a room when burned on charcoal. Lose rosemary leaves may be crushed in the hand and made into a course powder for this general use. It is a good incense for the bedroom of homes as it has a calming vibration. Giving someone a sachet filled with Rosemary is supposed to ensure friendship. The herb is also supposed to improve the memory.

Medicinally, it is used as a tonic for strengthening and toning the muscles. Its best culinary use is as a seasoning for lamb.

ROSEMARY POWDER   Used for blessing and purifying purposes. One of the most secret ingredients of some of the floor sweeping compounds used to cleanse a place.

RUE (Ruda)   The Perfume and oil come from the essential oil. Rue Water is made from a tea, and is used for a bath for purification. Rue is the primary herb of Christianity, and is used in a bath to end religious confusion in Christians. The herb itself may be used in a tea to induce abortion.

S

SAFFRON (Azafran) This is an incense used by some ceremonial magicians in some rituals. The best incense is made from pure saffron, and is quite expensive. In practice it is usually diluted at least 100:1 with Bamba wood or another filler. In the worst case, it is just a yellow dyed wood flour.

SANDALWOOD INCENSE Usually available either in chips of the wood, or in powder form. It is sometimes available either in little balls, or as a paste. It is the most common stick incense there is. It has the property of feeding and delighting the elemental entities. The wood is occasionally available for use in making chests and cabinets.

SANDALWOOD POWDER Used as a blow powder in elemental magic, it is made from pure sandalwood powder of the kind used in incense. Most elemental spirits love this powder, as well as the fumes of the incense. Also known as Chandan Powder, the Hindi name for Sandalwood.

SARSAPARILLA The original soda fountain drink, the herb is used for headaches, general feelings of ache and pain, as well as for treating colds and fevers. I have two spells using this herb but as I have never been able to obtain any, I have no idea if the spells are effective.

SASSAFRAS   Once one of North America's leading exports, as it was thought to be an All Heal. It is now a restricted drug, as the FDA says that it causes cancer. The tea is a nervine and calmative.   The incense of the root is used to calm nervous places.   The incense is good for calming children's play rooms kindergartens and child care centers.   It is not a banishing incense, but a general calmative. The powder of the root is the thickener used in Creole cooking, Gumbo File.

SATURN   (Saterno)   An incense made of Civet, Musk and Alum in a Yew or Ash wood powder base is good for summoning this planetary spirit.

SEAL OF VENUS OIL   (El Sello de Venus)   The seal is to be engraved on a copper disk on the day and hour of Venus. The disk must be placed in the bottle of the oil, which is to be made from the essential oil of Artissima. Some of the plant should be in the bottle as well.

SEPARATION POWDER   (Separacion)   A powder used to break up any kind of relationship.   The powder can create animosity, quarrels, and even fights between friends, lovers, business partners, and any others who are grouped together. The use of this powder in a spell forces an eventual separation. It is made from equal parts of castor bean powder and pomegranate root powder, mixed well and aged a month or so. The expediter for this powder, to make it work even faster is Asafetida and Cattail head powder. I recommend you judge the difficulty of the separation first, and then use the degree of strength desired immediately. This formula has been found to be quite effective in practice.

SEVEN DAY CANDLES,   SEVEN WAY CANDLES   Found in grocery stores in Latino neighborhoods, as well as in Botanicas and occult stores, these candles are burned as offerings to Saints and Orisha whose pictures are often glued or painted on the candle. The seven-way candle has seven layers of different colored wax in it. They are to be burned one layer

170

a day for seven days, using prayers appropriate to the color of the wax being burned.

SEVEN KNOB CANDLE   SEVEN NEEDLE CANDLE   The seven-knob candle is made with seven large knobs of wax on the body of the candle. One knob is to be burned each day for seven days to complete a spell.

The Seven-needle candle is made from a regular dinner candle, divided into eight sections. Seven needles are heated one at a time and forced into the candle, equally spaced apart. Once the seven-needle candle is completed it is to be burned each day until a needle falls out, Then it is to be snuffed out. These candles are used with a variety of spells, most of which are of the wishing variety.

SILVER LEAF   This is a plant whose leaf has a silver appearance, caused by a whitening of the leaf itself. Supposedly it is a good luck charm, but I have no idea what the plant actually is.

SHOE BLESSING POWDER   I was asked to make this up for a lady who wanted to walk in safety through a particularly nasty business meeting. I made up a small amount of parsley, cinnamon, and powdered iron filings, prayed over it for her, and gave the powder to her. She applied it to the inside of the shoes she was to wear to the meeting. She survived the meeting, although several of her associates lost their positions immediately following the meeting.

SHOESTRING ROOT POWDER   Made from powdered Devils Shoestring, which see.   This can be a powerful commanding powder. It must be fed with alcohol and charged with a prayer before use.

SNAKE OIL   (Vibora)   Used as a healing or a massage oil. This oil is rendered from snake fat. The best version of this oil is taken from a rainbow boa constrictor. The real oil is quite expensive. The oil is also used to anoint candles. The oil is usually diluted or even replaced by mineral oil. The snake oil used in serious work should be at least 51% snake oil to be effective for it's purpose. It is very difficult to obtain the real Rainbow Boa Oil.

SNUFF POWDER   Commercial snuff may be used as a blow powder to feed elemental spirits. It may also be used for laying hexes, for protecting a person, or for other work with the elemental forces. Some of the higher elemental spirits love this powdered tobacco product.

SOLOMON'S SPIRIT POWDER   (Solomons Holy Spirit Powder)   Made from pure ground Solomon's Seal herb. It is useful for working with mediums, as it may be used to restrict the quality of the spirit that is drawn to a medium.

SORTES SACRA   The Sacred Way   This refers to the primrose path, a specific occult practice. While it is supposedly an expediter for other spells, it is another name for a magical path used as the name of a product. The magical path is the western version of a sexual practice similar to the Indian Tantric Yoga. You will find it far easier to find a teacher of Tantric Yoga today than to find someone who will actually lead you down the primrose path, or on to the Sacred Way.

SPEARMINT   (Menta Verde)   Used in a number of spells like peppermint, which see. It is said to affect the mind, which it stimulates.

SPECIAL FAVORS OIL   (Favor Especial)   Used to attract and work with friendly elementals and nature spirits. Made of Cedar wood powder and Sandalwood, in a base of Cedar oil or turpentine. Best used outside, as an anointing oil on a tree or stone, but it may be used inside if you are careful.

Please do not make the mistake of thinking you can command these elemental beings. For success in working with them you must work in harmony with them.

SPIDER QUEEN OIL   A mineral oil based material that contains a dead spider. It is a power oil favored in Mexican Magical practices.

S

SPIKENARD   This was the herbal essence used to anoint Jesus Christ. It is used in love spells, and in many other forms of magic.   The sucess of the root is an excellent astral condenser. The tea is a good astral condenser, but not as good as Marigold flowers. The perfume is used in Christian magic, where the saints are prayed to.

SPIRITS, ALCOHOLIC   Aqua Vita means Water of life, it is at least 51% Ethyl Alcohol. (102 proof) Vodka is usually 80 to 100 proof. (40 to 50 % ethyl alcohol) The limit of alcohol that is reachable by distillation is about 90%. This is 180 proof, the practical limit of drinking alcohol. Rectified spirits is an alcohol that has been through another process following distillation. Rectified spirits are as close to pure alcohol as you can get.

Alchemical Alcohol is a triple distilled alcohol, usually made from Burgundy wine.   It is between 80% and 90 % Ethyl Alcohol. The first distillation usually yields about 40 % alcohol, 200 proof. The second distillation yields about 75% alcohol, 400 proof. The third distillation yields about 90% or a bit less alcohol, 600 proof. With Alchemical Alcohol, it is the source and the process, rather than the chemical proof of the alcohol, that gives it its great value in magical operations. (Chemically, pure alcohol is 200 proof)

STREGA   This is the name of an Italian witchcraft practice, and has no real relationship to any material product.   This is another case of a magical practice being used to name a series of product, like Sortes Sacra. There is a Strega Liquor however, which is a nice after dinner drink.

SUCCESS AND GOOD FORTUNE AT YOUR BUSINESS
(Truinfo en el Negocio)   Incense, Perfume and Floor wash
Mint, Honeysuckle, Parsley, and Cinnamon with a bit of Honey in it makes up the best floor wash, or rinse, for any business. It should be applied over a clean floor, something that seems to often be overlooked. You may add a couple of ounces of rum to the floor wash to make the effect stronger, but you should use this rinse only once a month. Pray over the bucket with the floor wash in it before using it.

Mint and Honeysuckle make the best business perfume, while Cinnamon and Frankincense make a good business incense. However you should use these incenses and perfumes lightly, or people will think you are too weird to do business with.

SWEET PEA   (Guisante Dulce)   Perfume, Powder, and Oil Made from the essential Oil.   By its own nature, it attracts people to the one wearing it.   This makes the best attraction perfume and oil there is.   A good bath powder for those who want to make a lot of friends.   You must be selective as to the people it attracts to you.

20

T

TAKING THE MEASURE   A rite practiced in witchcraft, which puts a trace of the member of the coven into the hands of the leader of the coven. Done in a variety of ways, it is not particularly dangerous to the person whose measure is being taken.

TAMING POWDER   (Amansar, Amansamiento, or Domesticado) The best product for taming others is made from the Palo Amansa Guapo which has been worked in accordance with the nature of the palo to tame others. An initiate must do this work, and such a product is very difficult to find.

TARRAGON   This kitchen spice added to chicken improves both the flavor and the healing qualities of the meal.

TAR PERFUME OIL   (Black Tar Oil) Cheaply made from roofing tar and Crisco oil. It is a thick black product that emulates the original. This is hardly a neat perfume, but it finds its uses in magic non-the less. The roofing tar may be used alone for almost as good a result. Used in a variety of spells besides cursing and blocking an enemy. Some people like this odor as a perfume, or an incense.

The product may be used to 'smear the reputation' of someone by applying it to their business card.

TETRAGAMMATON   The seventy-two letter name of God in Jewish Mysticism.   There is no one incense or oil that matches the nature of this name, thus all of the commercial products using this name are not valid.

THYME   Burn this kitchen spice as an incense in the home for health and luck.

TIBET   This former place of mystery now has regular tourist excursions to show its sights to the world.   A Chinese friend showed me a product called China Tibet Oil at a store in New York's Chinatown.   The product was a healing massage oil for strains and sprains.   There is no occult product named after Tibet that has any validity.

TIGER OIL   (Tigre)   A perfumed oil that supposedly awakens the psychic powers of the person to whom it is applied.   Some people believe commercial 'Tiger Balm' massage compound will do the same thing.   It will work as well as this oil.

TONKA BEAN OIL   (Haba Tonka)   Usually mineral oil with a tonka bean in the bottle.   Used in luck and protection spells.   Tonka beans are carried as good luck charms.

TRANQUIL   (Tranquillo)   Any minor sedative product, calming and relaxing the nervous system.   Try using Camomile tea for this purpose.

TRANQUILLITY POWDER   Used to overcome resistance, particularly nervous or mental resistance from others.   It is particularly good for the hypnotist or the trance inducer to use in calming subjects prior to induction.   It makes a fair incense, having about the same effect.

Made from Three parts Rose powder, One part Frankincense, Two parts Vetavert, One part Honeysuckle.   Mix the ingredients together and allow them to sit for at least a day (a full 24 hours) before using the powder.

T

TURQUOISE OIL   Supposedly a healing oil.   Usually Mineral oil put up in a bottle with a small piece of semi precious Turquoise stone in it.   Sunflower oil is better for the purpose. May be used for anointing candles for healing rituals.

TWISTING POWDER   This powder is made from the twisting tendrils of the grape vine. It takes an amazing charge, and will twist and tangle anything you place it on. It is especially useful in reversing spells that have been sent to someone. A Greek client recommended it to me many years ago, and I have used it successfully ever since. To get some of the tendrils, check your table grapes.

TYING THE NATURE   A spell used to restrict or deny a man the use of his sexual function. A Hoodoo spell used to 'tie the nature' of a man, preventing him from having sexual relations with another woman than the one who has 'Tied him,' or has 'Tied his nature.'   A very popular spell that married women often ask for.

21

U

UNCROSSING OIL (Discruza or Desenvolvimiento) Used to remove all kinds of hexes, jinxes, and crossed conditions. No one oil will suit all cases, so this wonder product, like many others, does not really exist. A thorough spiritual cleansing is suggested if this product is needed.

V

VALERIAN   A calmative tea, stronger than comfrey, and not as often recommended.   Some people hallucinate from the fumes when it is burned as an incense.

VANILLA   Made from cooking Vanilla, it is much used in love spells, both the essential oil and the imitation are useful in love and other spells.   The grocery store vanilla, whether pure or artificial, is an alcoholic vanilla extract, and may be used to make a good love perfume.   Also used to dress candles successfully, it takes a good charge magically.

At one time it was a favorite perfume of professional women.

VAN VAN OIL   [New Orleans Style, Algiers Style, Southern Style - they are all essentially the same product.]   An all-purpose dressing oil for candles and charms, it is also used in scrub water to wash out a place, or in baths to clear a person.

VERVAIN   (Verbena)   The enchanters herb, useful as an incense, for making oils, waters, baths, and powders.   This herb is useful in many ways, and every person interested in magical work should keep a little on hand. May be used in working with spirits, astral beings, or elementals for blessing, healing, cursing, and curing. Used in charm bags for both curing and protection.

VIOLET   Perfume oil, floor wash. Used to promote healing and bring money and health into the home. Carnation oil is better (and usually cheaper) for all of these tasks.

VOLADOR   (Do Away With)   Powdered Deer horn, it is added to mineral oil and used in spells forcing people to move, or at least to leave you alone. As a casting powder, it has the same effect.

VOODOO   Voudon (Vu Du)   The Voodoo practice is a complete magical religious practice. The religion utilizes any number of powders, oils, waters, gums, waxes, soaps, and so forth. There is no generic product that suits the very complex religion, just as there is no generic product that suits the entire Christian religion.

23

W

WAR WATER   (Agua de Guerra)   All of the various 'War' products contain Iron Oxide, which is rust. War Water is made from rust and water. Magically, it is essentially the essence of Iron in Water. It may be made from artist's Red Ocher, which is pure Iron Oxide. (FeO_2)

In rural traditional practice, War Water is made from water taken from the rain barrel and old cut (iron) nails. The water is allowed to become cloudy with rust. The cloudier it is, the stronger it is said to be.

War water is used in conducting magical wars, as well as being used in protection from them. The primary use of war water is in laying curses and in other spells directed against people. It is also used to break these spells. It may be used in a bath or applied to the body. It may also be used by pouring it across the doorway of the enemy, or by placing it in their path. It is derived from European practice, where it originated in the 1500's as a medicinal tonic product, known as Iron water. The tonic was used for treating Hysteria, which was considered a female complaint.

MATERIA MAGICA

WAR POWDER   Iron Oxide, known as Mars Red, or Ocher, is the main ingredient in this powder. Much depends on how it is made, and who makes it. Frequently just rust scraped from any rusty iron object. This powder is most often used for hexing and cursing an enemy. It becomes a potent weapon in any magical war.

Write the name of your enemy on a piece of scrap paper and coat it with war powder. Fold the paper into a packet, folding the paper away from yourself each time you fold it. Seal the packet all around, with red sealing wax. Then cast the packet into a river while cursing the one whose name is written inside.

An excellent War powder is made from five parts of Mars Red (Ocher) powder and two parts of magnetic sand. (Iron Filings) the powder should be prayed over, and cast with a curse on the steps of the enemy's home at night.

WISHING POWDER   Bay leaf powder or mullein herb powder usually diluted with Talc. It is used to make Wishes with

WISTERIA   Incense   Made from the essential oil and Winters Bark. Burn it at midnight to change your luck for the better.   A midnight fumigation with Wisteria incense by a spiritual worker will have a very positive effect on the person who has had a string of bad luck. This fumigation should always follow a full spiritual cleansing.

x

?

Y

YLANG YLANG   (Kananga) (Clang Ilang) [Cananga odorata]   An oil used for many purposes from the paint industry to the plastics industry. You can buy the diluted version by the quart at some paint stores. It is used to conceal the odor of drying paint.

Grown in Indonesia and Jamaica, the oil is a constituent of 'Florida Water.' It is used in treating excitable conditions, regulating the adrenaline flow, and relaxing the nervous system, resulting in a feeling of joy.'

YUZA YUZA OIL   Used to summon spirits of the dead, usually for cursing others. Made of wormwood and asafetida in mineral oil. Allow it age for at least a week before using. Place a small equal limbed cross of the oil at the place where you wish the curse to be laid, then pray over it the curse you wish to lay. It may be used to lay particularly evil curses at a particular location.

26

Z

ZORBA   Named after the fictional Zorba the Greek, it is a Damania herbal extract in an alcoholic base that is given to men to improve their sexual potency.   The commercial product is sold across the counter under this and several other brand names, such as El Toro, Macho, and others in Mexico.

53,270   Gr. 12.0

Printed in Great Britain
by Amazon

56484721R00112